with other basic responses in his conclusion. An appendix gives a survey of Gogarten's writings prior to and including the World War II period. This book should be a great help to those English-speaking theologians desiring to know more about this influential German thinker.

THE AUTHOR

LARRY SHINER is associate professor of religion at Cornell College, Mt. Vernon, Iowa.

He is a graduate of Northwestern University (B.A.), Drew University (B.D.), and the University of Strasbourg in France (Ph.D.). While in Strasbourg he visited with Professor Gogarten in Götingen, an experience which contributed much to this keen analysis of his work. A William S. Pilling Traveling Fellowship awarded by Drew enabled him to do his work in Strasbourg.

THE
SECULARIZATION OF
HISTORY

THE
SECULARIZATION OF
HISTORY An Introduction to
the Theology of Friedrich Gogarten

LARRY SHINER

ABINGDON PRESS   Nashville   New York

To the Memory of
Carl Michalson

Media morte in vita sumus

PREFACE

There can be no doubt that secularization and history are among the central themes of contemporary theology. The growing influence of Friedrich Gogarten's work can in part be traced to his having shown the profound interconnection of these two problems. Although he remains a significant contributor to the cutting edge of theological discussion, Gogarten is no newcomer. In a sense he has actually had two careers. The first was in the twenties and thirties as one of the co-founders, along with Karl Barth and Emil Brunner, of the "Dialectical Theology." The second was inaugurated just after the Second World War when Gogarten, then in his sixties, began to explore the problem of faith and history in the light of the phenomenon of secularization, a project that has continued down to the present. Gogarten's thought is becoming increasingly known in the English-speaking world not only through translations but also through the effectiveness of his teaching. In 1956 he went to Scotland where he lectured at the University of Glasgow, and in 1957-58 he spent a year in the United States as Visiting Professor at Drew University.

The scope of this study of Gogarten's work is intentionally introductory and does not aim at the kind of extensive treatment of particular concepts or themes possible in a monograph. It has not been feasible to make as full use of Gogarten's most recent book, *Jesus Christus Wende der Welt; Grundfragen der Christologie* (Jesus Christ Turning Point of the World, Fundamental Questions of Christology), as I would have liked, since it arrived when the manuscript was already in the production process. Nevertheless, I am grateful to Abingdon Press for permitting me to make a number of revisions in chapters III and IV. Since at present only two of Gogarten's works exist in translation, I have used the German versions of all his writings and made my own renderings.

The manuscript could never have been completed were it not for the encouragement and assistance of a number of people. Professor Gogarten gave generously of his time both at Drew and Göttingen and showed to me as to all his students that openness of which he writes so impressively. I am particularly grateful to him for reading the entire manuscript and making many valuable comments and suggestions. The criticism which my first work on Gogarten's thought received from Professors Roger Mehl and Étienne Trocmé of the Université de Strasbourg and Professor Gibson Winter of the University of Chicago has been of great value. I have also received helpful advice on several points from John Godsey of Drew University and from my Cornell colleagues Kenneth Freeman, Eric C. Kollman, and Thomas T. Love. I am especially indebted to my colleague James Goss, who read parts of the manuscript and made a number of valuable criticisms. To Bernard Richardson, Cornell librarian, I am most grateful for reading proof with me and offering many suggestions for stylistic improvements. And finally I cannot fail to acknowledge with deep gratitude all that I have learned from Carl Michalson, at whose counsel and inspiration the present work was undertaken.

Cornell College was good enough to provide a summer research grant which helped me complete the final stages of research. Mrs. Mary Byerly of the Russell D. Cole Library was particularly helpful in obtaining some of the materials I needed. The manuscript was typed by Mrs. Marianne Bern and Mrs. Stella Mae Easker. Throughout the vicissitudes of the project my wife's encouragement and assistance have immeasurably lightened the burden of writing.

Mt. Vernon, Iowa
April 27, 1966

LARRY SHINER

CONTENTS

Abbreviations 13

Introduction 17

I. *The Isolation of Man*
   1. The Christian Origin of Secularization 25
   2. "Christianity" and the Fate of Secularization .. 35
   3. Secular Man 42

II. *Historicity and the Hiddenness of God*
   1. The Question 50
   2. History 58
   3. The Hidden God 74

III. *The Humanity of Jesus Christ*
   1. The Historical Reality of Jesus 84
   2. The Preaching of Jesus 91

11

The Secularization of History

  3. The Responsibility of the Son 100
  4. Christological Formulation 105

IV. *The Reality of Faith*
  1. Faith and the Historical Reality of Jesus 118
  2. The Subjectivity of Faith 125
  3. Faith and Community 133
  4. Faith and Historical Research 136

V. *Secular Ethics*
  1. The Risk of Reason 147
  2. The Church and the World 160
  3. Secularization, Secularism, and Fate 165

VI *Gogarten and the Theology of Secularization Today* .. 174

  Appendix: Between the Times, 1914-1948 191

  Bibliography 223
  Index 229

ABBREVIATIONS

EK   *Entmythologisierung und Kirche,* 2 Aufl., Stuttgart, 1953. (English translation, *Demythologizing and History,* New York, 1955, tr. Neville Horton Smith. Based on first German edition.)

JCWW   *Jesus Christus Wende der Welt,* Tübingen, 1966.

KW   *Die Kirche in der Welt,* Heidelberg, 1948.

MZGW   *Der Mensch zwischen Gott und Welt,* Stuttgart, 1956.

VH   *Verhängnis und Hoffnung der Neuzeit,* Stuttgart, 1953.

VJC   *Die Verkündigung Jesu Christi,* Heidelberg, 1948.

WG   *Die Wirklichkeit des Glaubens,* Stuttgart, 1957. (English translation, *The Reality of Faith,* Philadelphia, 1959, tr. Carl Michalson and others.)

WIC   *Was ist Christentum?* Göttingen, 1956.

ZThK   *Zeitschrift für Theologie und Kirche.*

THE
SECULARIZATION OF
HISTORY

INTRODUCTION

"Secular" Christianity is the mode. Clerical anti-clerical-ism and theological anti-theology now appear alongside the anti-hero and the anti-novel. Yet most of our current theological efforts toward a nonreligious Christianity are as programmatic as Bonhoeffer's were. And where we have managed to get beyond the projection stage the results sound strangely like some of the things Henry Nelson Wieman said thirty years ago, now with the added pathos of the "death of God" motif. This not too impressive showing might suggest that if secularization is in fact the prime mark of our religious situation, a depth sounding is needed lest we leap into a too shallow solution.

It is toward such an analysis that the work of Friedrich Gogarten directs us. That this older theologian (b. 1887) may have something to teach us about secularity will not surprise those who remember that along with Barth and Brunner

The Secularization of History

Gogarten was writing of the worldliness of the Christian man when Bonhoeffer was still a university student.[1] Yet like Bonhoeffer, Gogarten was brought to the full vision of a secular Christian faith by national socialism and the war.[2] In a series of occasional works since 1948 he has developed a many-sided theological appraisal of secularization, whose central thesis identifies secularization as the logical and appropriate outcome of the responsibility for the world bestowed on man by faith. The corollary of this faith-sponsored secularization is the historicizing of human existence—since a historical mode of existence in Gogarten's view is determined by whether man is responsible for his own destiny. Thus although nearly all contemporary theologians affirm that Christianity is distinguished by its roots in history, Gogarten makes the connection between faith and history a whole octave deeper. What gives his writings particular relevance to the theological discussion of the moment is not simply that secularization is his explicit theme, but that he has endeavored to think through the problem of theology and history exclusively within the context of secularization. In Germany Gogarten's work has been particularly influential among the "post-Bultmannians," especially Gerhard Ebeling and Ernst Fuchs.[3] His influence on American

[1] Friedrich Gogarten, *Illusionen* (Jena, 1926), pp. 139 ff. The outstanding characteristic of the Protestant man's life style, he wrote, is its "radical worldliness." (*Ibid.*) This worldliness means the Christian remains only a man—not a special type or form of man—but simply a man. (*Ibid.*, pp. 144-45.) One cannot help being struck by the similarity to Bonhoeffer's letters where he, too, writes of the worldliness of the Christian man who is not a saint or a *homo religiosus* but simply a man. (*Prisoner for God* [New York, 1957], p. 166. Or: *Letters and Papers from Prison* [New York: Macmillan Paperbacks Ed., 1962], p. 95.) What was missing in Gogarten's earlier work, however, was his positive appraisal of the efforts of the *secular* man to maintain this worldliness, and his understanding of the Christian origin of the secularization of the world.

[2] See Appendix.

[3] See especially Ernst Fuchs, *Begegnung mit dem Wort* (Bad Cannstatt, 1955). (This was the address on the occasion of Gogarten's becoming professor emeritus.) Works by Fuchs where Gogarten's influence is espe-

18

theology can be immediately seen in Harvey Cox's *The Secular City* for which Gogarten's concept of the Christian origin of secularization provides part of the basic theological framework, and in Carl Michalson's efforts to do theology *as* history on the basis of a phenomenologically derived distinction between nature and history.[4]

Gogarten believes the need for thinking through the implications of a secular historical consciousness is nowhere more urgent today than in Christology. The prevalence in the "salvation history" theologies of terms like "God acts *in* history" or revelation "breaks *into* history" indicates how half-hearted our effort to think historically has really been. The "fact-meaning" dichotomy so widely assumed ties revelation to history the way one ties a name tag to a geological specimen, but Gogarten sees the problem as one of expressing revelation itself, the divine itself *as* history. Thus he can write that "where revelation occurs, nothing but history occurs." [5]

The consequences of his conviction that secularization originates in Christian faith itself are equally radical for ethics. Our new-found embrace of the "worldly" has given much of contemporary theology a predisposition for contextualism, but at the same time it has reinforced a powerful drive to get the church into the forefront of social change. The resulting confusion has led many to suggest we cannot simply immerse ourselves in the context and wait for its "demand" to appear, but must work out some form of natural law or biblical ethic. The consistent solution, as Gogarten sees it, is to get the church

---

cially apparent are *Hermeneutik* (Bad Cannstatt, 1954 and 1958), pp. 73-89, and *Zum hermeneutischen Problem in der Theologie* (Tübingen, 1959). For Ebeling mention must be made of *Word and Faith* (Philadelphia, 1963), and *The Nature of Faith* (Philadelphia, 1961). See also *Theologie und Verkündigung* (Tübingen, 1962), which is dedicated to Gogarten, p. viii.

[4] Harvey Cox, *The Secular City* (New York, 1965). Carl Michalson, *The Hinge of History* (New York, 1959), and *The Rationality of Faith* (New York, 1963).

[5] ZThK, 1953, p. 342.

out of the direct business of ethics entirely. Here is where his version of a secular theology clashes most sharply with other efforts to meet the secular challenge—like those of Hamilton or Van Buren who tend to reduce the meaning of faith to its ethical dimensions.[6]

As the foregoing samples of his position on Christology and ethics suggest, Gogarten's entire postwar work may be seen as an effort to create a theology within the limits of the finite. With determined opposition to metaphysics in the sense of thinking in terms of two worlds (natural/supernatural, historical/superhistorical), he has moved ever deeper into the implications of a strictly historical theology. So thoroughly has he carried out the implication of the Christian origin of secularization that a conservative Lutheran critic has called his work "The Gospel of Secularization." [7] But secularization is far more than a mere catchword; it is a sign of hope and fatality which demands a radical reconditioning of the entire theological enterprise, an effort which cannot be the achievement of one man or even of one generation. The real usefulness of his work is its exploratory character. He has probed the key problems of secularization and history in a unique and original way, and not hesitated to follow the implications of his new insights to the end. Gogarten would be the last to claim he had achieved the decisive breakthrough on a question which has exercised theology for the last two hundred years. On the contrary, he is always beginning anew, seeking various vantage points for penetration, cutting new paths into the tangled thicket of secularized Christendom.

[6] William Hamilton, *The New Essence of Christianity* (New York, 1961). Also by Hamilton, "The Death of God Theologies Today," *The Christian Scholar,* Spring, 1965, pp. 27-48. Paul Van Buren, *The Secular Meaning of the Gospel* (New York, 1963).

[7] Regin Prenter, "Das Evangelium der Säkularisierung," *Theologische Zeitschrift,* 1956, pp. 605 ff.

Gogarten is still best known to the English-speaking world, however, as the author of one of the most influential defenses of Bultmann (*Demythologizing and History*, 1953) and consequently is sometimes referred to as the systematic theologian of the "Existentialist" school.[8] Unfortunately the brevity of *Demythologizing and History* and the polemical context in which it was written did not permit many of Gogarten's significant themes to come to the fore. The publication of *The Reality of Faith* in 1959 has done much to fill in the picture of his work, but here again the book is directed at a particular problem—subjectivism—and cannot be read as a balanced presentation of his thought. But even when translations of his larger and more comprehensive works appear, a further difficulty faces the reader approaching Gogarten for the first time. Carl Michalson drew attention to this in the preface he wrote for *The Reality of Faith* when he warned that Gogarten "conceives his theology almost symphonically" and that his literary strategy emulates a detective story in which the most important clues are withheld until the moment when they will most effectively further the plot.[9] Readers less appreciative of Gogarten's basic

---

[8] John MacQuarrie, *Twentieth-Century Religious Thought* (New York, 1963), pp. 364-65. There has been an increasing convergence between Bultmann and Gogarten on many issues since the mid-1920's, although it is only in Gogarten's writings published since 1952 that Bultmannian terminology has been prominent. The intellectual and personal kinship of the two men is so close and of such long standing that it is almost impossible to say who borrowed what and when. See Bultmann's 1930 essay "The Historicity of Man and Faith," in Bultmann, *Existence and Faith* (New York, 1960), p. 102. It is no surprise, then, that Gogarten should have immediately allied himself with the demythologizing program (cf. VJC, pp. 451-53) and entered the controversy at its height with a defense of Bultmann, or that Bultmann should remark in 1956 that while his own concern with philosophy had brought him increasingly into opposition with Karl Barth, the "community of theological intentions between Gogarten and myself has become more and more apparent" (*Existence and Faith*, p. 288).

[9] Carl Michalson in the Translator's Preface to *The Reality of Faith* (New York, 1959), p. 8.

position might be inclined to think his turgid style merely reflects the renowned teutonic penchant for "profundity" at the expense of clarity, and it must be admitted that some of the difficulty in understanding Gogarten derives from his own failure to marshall his arguments in a way that leaves the fundamental concepts in bold relief. Nevertheless, the very nature of what he seeks to think through repels the possibility of a neat conceptual synthesis whose meaning is readily available on the surface. Basically he is trying to describe what it means to *be* a Christian in a "world come of age," and the very simplicity of this mode of being means that terms like freedom, openness, courage, faith resonate together whenever any one of them is sounded. The purpose of this introductory study of his work, therefore, is neither to repeat his own style in English nor to reduce its resonance to "clear and distinct ideas," but to provide the reader with a sketch of its major themes, to show their interrelationship, and to suggest some avenues of appropriate criticism. Although each chapter is devoted to a separate theme, I have tried to incorporate a logical development as the discussion proceeds. Thus the basic theological method and the anthropological structure underlying his work is unfolded through the first two chapters, which deal with the problems of secularization and of history respectively, and this foundation is presupposed in the chapters on Christology, faith, and ethics which follow. The critical questions and comments at the end of each chapter and in the conclusion make no pretence of raising all the relevant issues, but hopefully they may aid in setting in relief the salient features of Gogarten's theological encounter with secularization. Since there is an important shift in his attitude toward secularization during the decade surrounding the Second World War (1937-1947), it has seemed wise to concentrate on his postwar works where secularization is the dominant and pervasive theme. Nevertheless, the continuity between the two periods is such that the earlier work will be mentioned in the text from time to time in order to clarify certain aspects of his recent thought, and a survey of his theological development from 1914 to 1948 is offered in an appendix.

I

THE ISOLATION OF MAN

1

The Christian Origin of Secularization

The term "secularization" first appeared in a sense approximating its contemporary usage at the writing of the Treaty of Westphalia where it designated lands transferred from the church to the princes.[1] Its connotations at the time were neutral and no more anti-Christian than the term "secular clergy." Gradually secularization came to be applied to any aspect of life that was withdrawn from the control of the church or interpreted apart from the Christian world view. Today we retain

[1] For an excellent discussion of the history of the term secularization, see Martin Stallmann, *Was ist Säkularisierung?* (Tübingen, 1960), pp. 5-17.

this sense of the word when referring to the capitalist spirit as a secularization of the Puritan ethos or to Marxism as a secularized Judeo-Christian eschatology, etc. The essential element here, according to Gogarten, is the transformation of institutions, ideas, and experiences that were once the work of divine providence into the product of purely human thought and action.[2]

Although Gogarten uses this definition of secularization as a reflection of the spiritual transformation of the West over the last seven hundred years, he is convinced the divorce of Western culture from its religious foundation could never have occurred if man had not *already* become independent of the supernatural powers of the cosmos. The deeper meaning of secularization for Gogarten, therefore, is not the obvious change in "ideas" or the revolt against "organized religion," but the coming to fruition of a transformed relation to the world. At the heart of this permutation is man's emergence from subservience under cosmic forces into a relationship of responsibility for the world. By the time we reach the "modern" period Western man has become "mature" in the sense that he universally experiences responsibility for his own destiny as the *task* set by his relation to the world. However feebly we may live up to it, Gogarten sees in this responsibility the Law before which we must justify ourselves today, the ultimate "ought" written into the fabric of existence.[3] When compared to this more fundamental transformation, "secularization" in the sense of breaking off the real or imagined shackles of the church or the "Christian world view" is an important but secondary phenomenon. Although Gogarten admits that the proximate source of modern secularity is to be found in such factors as Renaissance individualism and the rise of science, he believes the remote and primordial root

[2] VH, p. 7.
[3] Gogarten also speaks of it as an ethos of "maturity" or "freedom." MZGW, pp. 194 ff.

of secularization is the desacralization of the world through Christian faith. He builds his case for the Christian origin of secularization, therefore, on the contrast between the relation to the world of the Christian and the pre-Christian man.

The world of pre-Christian man is described by Gogarten as a mythically understood cosmos determining and securing human life by its spiritual powers. In this "mythical" relation to the world man is not really conscious of a world over against himself but lives in an immediate unity with the cosmos. Since history is possible only where man is responsible for what happens, the mythical experience is by nature ahistorical.[4] Gogarten grants that man's cosmic innocence did begin to dissolve with those Greeks who articulated an awareness of separation from the world. Whereas the battle of Troy is still conceived mythically with the divine and human action as one, for example, the battle of the Greeks and Persians is a history where only men are fighting and on their own responsibility. Yet as Gogarten points out, history for the Greeks is never the whole of reality but only the unceasing flux of the earthly above which reposes the unchanging divine cosmos.[5]

The definitive break with the mythical relation to the world, according to Gogarten, occurred in the prophetic preaching of Judaism and Christianity. He illustrates his case primarily with the writings of Paul who was explicitly concerned with the contrast between the old and new existence. Paul announces the end of the old cosmic order in his statement that through

---

[4] VJC, pp. 439-53. Georges Gusdorf makes a similar point in his essay, "Mythe, Raison, Histoire" *L'Homme et l'histoire* (Paris, 1952). Myth, reason, and history are modes of *présence au monde*. The mythical consciousness generates a spontaneous kind of behavior, of which the stories and legends are more or less feeble echoes. There is created here a horizon of thought whose limits are the world itself. "Man experiences himself in an immediate liaison with the environment, a single existence animating living beings and things" (*ibid.*, p. 303). This is manifestly a different concept of "myth" than the one behind Bultmann's "demythologizing" project.

[5] VJC, pp. 442-46.

Christ we have become mature sons who are free from the *stoicheia,* the ordering powers of the world (Gal. 4:1-11). Since these powers were considered divine, it is no accident that the early Christians were charged with atheism when they claimed the divinity had gone out of the world. Even the distinction between sacred and profane was swept aside, and meat from the sacrifices at pagan altars was in no way tainted, because those altars had been neutralized.[6] As a result not only did the Christian become self-conscious over against the world but once the canopy of the cosmos was pierced he was able to stand before the divine power as a person. For Gogarten the distinctiveness of the "new man" who emerges through Christian faith is his knowing of himself as person in relation to God and the world, a knowledge in which he is at once the independent master of his own destiny and receives his freedom in openness to the divine mystery.

If we are to grasp the full significance of Gogarten's argument for the secularizing and historicizing influence of Christian faith, an understanding of his concept of personhood is decisive. Basic for all Gogarten's work is his notion that human nature is a unity of receptivity and activity. As a receiver man is defined by his openness to other men and to the mystery of his being in the world. But as an active self-knowing agent man is able to stand by himself either accepting the fact that his life is bound up with that of others, or asserting his independence of them. Each of these dimensions is essential to the other if man is to exist as a person. To accept the fact that one's being is received from his relation to others and to the mystery of existence is at the same time to respond as one who can give or withhold himself. Yet there can be no genuine responsibility unless there has been a "call" from another. If this is true in everyday conversation, then

[6] WIC, p. 17.

it is especially true of a speaking in which man himself comes to expression, in which he pledges himself to someone—as in the language of love. Here the being of man speaks. In this re-sponding, man is free in his very essence for the other, and in the freedom of this re-sponse which is grounded in the speech of the other, he receives his being from him.[7]

This understanding of "response" and the corresponding responsibility *before* another can also be illustrated by considering its Latin root *spondere* which actually means "to pledge one's word" and in that sense to pledge oneself.

Gogarten calls this language in which a man pledges or imparts himself an "immediate word" as distinguished from language used as a "means" of conveying information, arousing emotions, directing action, etc. Of course an immediate word may not take the form of sound waves, since a gesture or movement, even the presence of another person, "speaks" to us and demands our presence for him. This notion of an immediate word—which Gogarten develops from the "Thou-I" motif of his earlier work—is not only conceived as the proper *analogy* for the "Word of God" but also as a *participant* in it. This is true both because the "Word" is spoken in the man Jesus of Nazareth and because man's relation to his fellowmen always directly involves his relation to God.[8]

According to Gogarten, the active side of personhood is constituted by the responsibility *for* the world which gives man the freedom to respond to the mystery of his being or to shut himself against it. The concept of "world" which Gogarten uses here refers to the "lived world," the complex of meanings,

---

[7] WG, pp. 48-49 (Eng. tr., pp. 50-51). Although in this passage Gogarten is making a play on *entsprechen* (usually translated "to correspond to"), the word he normally employs for "responsibility" is *Verantwortlichkeit* which permits a similar play on "word" (*Wort*) and "response" (*Antwort*). For his earlier discussion of responsibility in terms of the "Thou-I" motif, see below pp. 61-65 and 199-206.

[8] KW, p. 96.

relationships, institutions, and "things" which form the particular world of each man as well as the shared cultural world.
But the chief feature of "world" which gives it a pivotal
position in the problematic of secularization is the fact that
there can be no world at all without a coherence, without an
order or law. Even beatniks and Zen masters live by the
sort of law Gogarten is talking about—an elemental coherence
of life without which human existence would not be possible
whatever the adhesive may be: spontaneity, authenticity, un-
trammeled freedom, or the moments of perfect liaison between
man and woman.[9] In the pre-Christian world the order of
life is given as an eternal cosmic power which no man can violate
without the wrath of the gods descending on his head and
household. By depotentiating these cosmic forces and liberating man from their encompassing power, faith frees man
from bondage to the world and makes him responsible for its
coherence.

The fact that Gogarten believes this personhood first became historically effective through Christian faith does not
mean he regards it as something added to human nature. On
the contrary, the importance of his concept of personhood for an
understanding of the Christian origin of secularization actually
hinges on seeing it as the content of the "image of God" which
has been distorted but not lost through the Fall. Gogarten
distinguishes two senses of the image of God in man: one as in
Gen. 1:26, which is a formal likeness to God, an active capacity
belonging to man in his rule over the "creatures," and another
sense of the image as in II Cor. 3:18, where Paul says that

[9] "Man's life," Gogarten writes, "must be lived in an ordered structure
and a binding connection, if it is to remain human. This order and bond
is not a matter of course, otherwise human life would be a natural process
rather than a history. This order must unceasingly be preserved, better,
be wrenched, from the threat of chaos." (MZGW, p. 82.) Gogarten regards
the biblical commandments as historical forms of this order or law valid for
the Hebrew and early Christian communities but not binding on us.

"because for us there is no veil over the face, we all reflect as in a mirror the splendour of the Lord" (NEB). This reflected image is not a similarity to God's rule over the creatures but the image man receives when he lets himself be "known" by the divine mystery. The unity of the two images is expressed by Gogarten as man's knowing and caring for himself and the world in the awareness that he himself is known and cared for by God. He is the image of God in the active sense because he is responsible for the world and therefore does the "works of God" in the world; he is the image of God in the reflected sense because he does not have his coherence as person through what he does in the world, but by receiving his selfhood in openness to the divine counterpart.[10]

According to Gogarten, the "fall" or "sin" which distorts this twofold image is man's flight from worldly responsibility before God into a religious reverence before the "law" or "powers" he believes to order the world—or, in the language of Paul, it is the worship of the creature in the place of the Creator. When a man turns to receive his being from the world instead of from God, the things for which he was originally given responsibility come to have power over him as the object of his reverence. It is here that Gogarten finds the source of the pre-Christian bondage to the powers, since without the knowledge of his true counterpart a man becomes a worshiper of the cosmos and can no longer be responsible for the world because he has become responsible *before* it.[11] Two things about this notion of the distortion of the image through sin are of particular importance for Gogarten's idea of the Christian origin of secularization. First, sin is not a denial of the supernatural or of a set of divine laws, but in fact the height of religious reverence and slavish obedience before the ordering

---

[10] MZGW, pp. 331-33.
[11] WG, pp. 67-68 (Eng. tr., pp. 68-69), and VH, pp. 39 ff.

powers of the cosmos. Second, sin is in no sense the beginning of history but actually a flight from historical responsibility.

It follows that the restoration of man to his true humanity by Christian faith cannot mean for Gogarten the beginning of a sanctification of the world, but the very opposite—the secularization of the world and the liberation of man for full responsibility in the world. If man is brought from the death of captivity to the supernatural powers into the life of freedom for God and the world, he will be wrenched out of the cosmic enclosure and reflected back on himself in awareness of his total impotence before the mystery of existence.[12] In this radical reflectedness a new dimension of existence will be bestowed on him: he achieves an individuality and autonomy that was impossible in the sacral cosmos and only partially realized in the fate-laden experience of the Greeks.

Yet we must look closer still at the character of this restored responsibility if we are to feel the full impact of Gogarten's case for the secularization of the world through faith. The first thing Gogarten emphasizes about this responsibility is that it is always united with the knowledge that man's own being and the being of the world are received from beyond himself. He will not care for the world as a mere caretaker, but as a son cares for his patrimony in remembrance of the one who cared for him in creating it. This filial self-understanding does not interfere with his independence as the mature son, but it surrounds his autonomy with the kind of attentive concern for the heritage which only a grateful heir can experience. Here is the point where Gogarten's insistence on the secularity of the Christian life achieves its most radical results. Since the Christian is no

---

[12] "In faith in the God who makes alive the dead, there is opened up the deepest, most comprehensive reflection of man that is possible for him, a reflection in which he comes into view twice as a whole man." (MZGW, p. 173.)

longer a child but a mature son, he receives no directions as to *what* he is to do.

Gogarten's favorite text for expounding this radical maturity of the Christian man is Galatians 4:1-5:

This is what I mean: so long as the heir is a minor, he is no better off than a slave, even though the whole estate is his; he is under guardians and trustees until the date fixed by his father. And so it was with us. During our minority we were slaves to the elemental spirits of the universe, but when the term was completed, God sent his own Son, born of a woman, born under the law, to purchase freedom for the subjects of the law, in order that we might attain the status of sons. (NEB)

Gogarten points out that Paul counts the particular Jewish laws among the elemental spirits from which we are liberated when the son bestows maturity on all who become fellow heirs with him. Yet the end of the law in Jesus does not mean for Paul that it is abolished, but only that its religious power over man is broken. The law in its essence is still the eternal will of God, the will which makes only *one* demand: the person of man. This is why it is possible for Paul to say, "no man is justified before God by the law" at the same time he is saying that "the doers of the law will be justified." [13] The law is fulfilled when man receives his being from God. The decision as to what particular works should or should not be done is given over to man's own judgment. Paul can even accept the phrase: "all is permitted." Gogarten says of this:

However minor the external occasion on which Paul spoke the phrase: "all is permitted" it is nevertheless one of the most powerful words ever spoken. Because this statement opens up a fully new relation of man to the world, the face of the world has been completely changed. With this word the basis is laid for the lordship

[13] VH, pp. 75-85.

33

over the world and its powers that the human spirit is later to achieve.[14]

The basic notion in Gogarten's understanding of the Christian origin of secularization is that man is liberated from the encompassing power of the cosmos through the restoration of his twofold responsibility as a mature son. The "maturity" points to the fact that he exercises this responsibility in complete independence, relying solely on his own rational capacity; the "sonship" points to the fact that he exercises this responsibility in the context of receiving his being as a person in openness to God and his fellowmen.

Gogarten often describes this desacralization of the world as a movement from a mythical to a historical relation to the world, so that the secularization inaugurated by Christian faith is synonymous with historicization. Of course, there was history long before Christianity or even the Hebrew prophets and redactors. But although there was recorded human action whose echo has come down to us in codes, chronicles, inscriptions, and artifacts, Gogarten thinks that the man of pre-Christian times, with the exception of the Jews and, to a limited extent, the Greeks, did not *experience* the world historically, since to experience the world as history demands two attitudes which parallel the double dimensionality of personhood. First, we can only speak of man's existing historically when he is consciously responsible for his own destiny and that of the world, and where he therefore regards this sphere of ordinary human being and action as fully real. Secondly, man only exists historically when his responsibility for the world occurs in the context of a quest for the unity or meaning of history, a quest without which responsibility is either stultified by the acceptance of a prematurely final meaning or dissolved into the ritualism of mythical or technological process.

[14] *Ibid.*, pp. 97-98.

The connection between secularization and history is particularly important for Gogarten's work since he often speaks of the secularization of history even though he equates secularization and historicization in other passages.[15] The puzzle is easily solved if we keep in mind his two definitions of secularization: on the one hand it means the transformation of the relation between man and the world from a mythical unity with the cosmos to responsibility for the world; on the other hand it means the separation of originally Christian ideas and experiences from their divine ground and their transformation into purely human phenomena. The secularization and historicization which originate through Christian faith are obviously of the first kind. But once this secularization has taken place it is possible for the dimension of responsibility for the world to be separated from openness to the divine mystery with the result that we have a secularization of history or, cumbersome as it sounds, a secularization of Christian secularity. This secondary secularization by which man's independence is divorced from his acknowledgment of the divine mystery is, of course, what is often meant by the term "secularization" today.

2

"Christianity" and the Fate of Secularization

Gogarten grants that it took this secondary, anticlerically motivated secularization to actually make effective the desacralization of the world originally achieved by Christian faith. Neither the church of the post-Constantinian era nor the church of the Middle Ages can be said to have championed the maturity and independence of man. This would seem to raise a considerable difficulty for Gogarten's thesis of a Christian origin for secularization. Why is it that the Christian leap into history seems to have been arrested in its infancy? Why did seculariza-

[15] Cf., for example, VH, p. 103, and MZGW, p. 411.

tion as we know it need to incubate for over fifteen hundred years until the Enlightenment gave it a decisive push? And why, if secularization is so compatible with Christian faith, did the church resist man's responsibility for the world when it finally came to flower? Gogarten's answer will seem uncomfortably Protestant and Lutheran to many. He blames secularization's delay on the marriage of Christian faith with Hellenistic philosophy, a marriage whose incompatibility resulted in a well-advised divorce presided over by Martin Luther. Although Luther revived and extended the Pauline notion of man's maturity and responsibility for the world, his breakthrough was soon forgotten, and the church embarked on its battle with human independence, especially as expressed in science, and forced men to choose between "Christianity" as a divinely revealed world view and the ethos of an independent search for the truth. Although Gogarten has never offered a detailed analysis of this development, it will be illuminating to bring together his scattered remarks and fit them into a coherent picture of the fate of secularization.

According to Gogarten, one of the reasons secularization was delayed was the simple fact that the church had to fight for centuries to neutralize the divine powers as personified in sorcery, demons, etc., and in the process these many gods and spirits entered the church herself under various guises. So long as the church had to devote her main efforts to missionary work and to preventing the inundation of Christian faith by paganism, she had no time to develop the positive side of man's responsibility for the world.[16] More important in stifling the secularizing force of faith, however, was the fact that the church also remained under the sway of the classical understanding of man's relation to the world. One of the first monstrosities resulting from this all-too-holy alliance between Hellenistic

[16] WG, p. 85 (Eng. tr., p. 86).

philosophy and Christian faith was the figural or typological interpretation of history. The church fathers treated the Hebrew tradition as a succession of figures prognosticating the appearance of Christ, but the connection between the figures was not temporal or causal but vertical through the plan set by divine Providence (e.g., the link between the sacrifice of Isaac and that of Christ). Although the figural interpretation overcame the fatalism of classical literature, it submerged the unique realism of the New Testament. In contrast to classical writing which was able to express the realism of everyday life only in the lower style of comedy or satire, the New Testament elevated events occurring among fishermen and prostitutes to world transforming importance. But the figural interpretation, by linking these everyday events to an otherworldly plan smothered their historicity.[17] Gogarten finds an even fuller rationale for the figural interpretation achieved in Scholastic theology where the world was viewed as a natural reality within a supernatural, preestablished order. Immersed in a network of teleologically motivated substances, man could not be ultimately responsible for his destiny, and a historical existence in the genuine sense was impossible. In effect the medieval church transformed Christian faith into a world view that it hoped would provide the basis for a stable order, but the price paid for this magnificent achievement was to turn the mystical body

[17] Gogarten, "Das abendländische Geschichtsdenken" (ZThK, 1954), 330-36. This article is a discussion of Erich Auerbach's *Mimesis* (New York, 1957). What Gogarten finds most suggestive in *Mimesis* is Auerbach's indication of the way history emerges as *the* reality for Western man. According to Auerbach, the figural interpretation begins to fade out in Dante, who set men and women of such earthly passion in the "other" world that they break through the assigned stations of the divine economy. From this time on, Western literature turns ever more decisively toward the human; and there eventually unfolds that modern realism for which the individual human life, no matter how low its class position or base its character, is real. The whole human life thereby becomes historical.

into an encompassing power similar to the pre-Christian cosmos.[18]

In Luther Gogarten sees the freedom of the Christian man again radically affirmed as it had not been since Paul. In fact he believes Luther is the first one in the church to begin working out the implications of the secularization that occurred in the Cross. Consequently it is to Luther we should turn to see the inauguration of a theology whose categories are primarily historical rather than metaphysical. For Luther the freedom of man for God apart from the sacramental system of the church also carried with it a freedom for the world. The New Testament writers knew of this positive freedom, Gogarten explains, but their attention was directed primarily toward the freedom *from* the gods, demons, powers, and laws to which they had been subject. In Luther's situation, however, the church itself had become a cosmic power standing between God and man, so that the freedom Luther had to fight for is not so much the right of the individual conscience as the freedom of man to approach God. But if the cosmos—in its ecclesiastic-sacramental form—ceases to determine man's relation to God, then his relation to the world will also be free from the "Christian law." Luther expressed the double freedom of the Christian man in his doctrine of the two kingdoms. In Gogarten's view this doctrine is not only one of his greatest contributions to theology, but indispensable to an understanding of the relation of faith and secularization. For by denying the church's claim to sovereignty over the world, Luther turned the entire exterior aspect of man's life over to the dominion of human reason.[19]

[18] EK, pp. 30-33 (Eng. tr., pp. 21-24) ; WG, pp. 85-86 (Eng. tr., pp. 86-87).

[19] VK, pp. 405-6. Gogarten believes Luther carried secularization a step further than Paul, due to the difference in the nature of the law each was facing. For Paul the gospel finally puts an end to the Jewish legal piety and its particular demands. But for Luther the law in which he had sought his salvation was in fact the gospel, but understood as law by the church and used as law by him to justify himself. Therefore Luther did not battle

This great initiative, Gogarten laments, was soon lost since those who followed Luther allowed confessional combats to turn justification by faith into an article of belief. Before long the Protestant churches were battling the claims of independence and freedom put forth by science and throwing up a desperate rearguard defense of a biblical-Aristotelian world view. Since the churches were hurling divine law at science, it appealed to a law of its own which had emerged out of the exaltation of the creative individual in Renaissance humanism. With Descartes's *cogito* the new understanding of man achieved its most striking formula: the one thing certain is man himself. When this understanding of man as the free individual merged with science's drive to expand human control over nature (e.g., Bacon), a new authority appeared over against the Church—man himself in his autonomous responsibility.[20] Nevertheless, science in its actual research and theorizing has been able to remain largely free of ideological commitments, and Gogarten views its patient and fearless investigation, therefore, as the clearest expression of the freedom from the cosmic powers that was originally made available to mankind by Christian faith.

Gogarten blames the stultification of the secularization inaugurated by faith on the church whose highest task was to preserve the independence of man from cosmic powers. The real failure of the church, as Gogarten sees it, was not simply to have neglected this task, but to have headed in the opposite direction until it transformed *Christian faith* which is a mode of

---

against the law as such but against the *opinio,* man's intention to make himself just before God by fulfilling the law (MZGW, pp. 174-75). Because Luther started from the unity of law and gospel, he spoke of two uses of the law. The use which relates to the eternal salvation of man by driving him to Christ was the same as for Paul, but the use of the law by man's reason to guide his earthly life as God's creature is Luther's decisive contribution to secularization (*ibid.,* p. 207).

[20] VJC, pp. 406-8.

existence in "mature sonship" into *Christianity,* a supposedly revealed world view. Despite its effort to become a cosmic power encompassing man's freedom, the church has not been able to undo the desacralization originally effected by faith. Gogarten believes that once man had been given independence from supernatural forces and experienced his responsibility for the world, this new relation to the world becomes available to every man whether he is a believer or not. In the light of the church's having turned the freedom of faith into the world view we call Christianity, it is not surprising that more of the substance of Christian freedom is found outside the churches than within.

Since this distinction between Christian faith and Christianity is central for Gogarten, we should look at it more closely. "Christianity" embodies two misunderstandings of Christian faith, one moralistic, the other metaphysical. The moralistic misunderstanding of faith treats it as providing a pattern for man's action, so that instead of risking one's existence in faith one is commanded to believe this "Christian" pattern to be true and revealed by God.[21] The metaphysical misunderstanding comes closer to leaving room for genuine faith since it admits that man's wholeness is realized by God. But it cannot do justice to man's personhood, Gogarten believes, because it conceives the relation to God in naturalistic categories derived from the Hellenistic dualism of the spiritual world of being and the merely physical world of becoming and passing away.[22] When modern science destroyed the last props of the supernatural world, Christianity came to be seen strictly in moralistic terms by the historians and philosophers of religion and by the "liberal" theologians who adopted their viewpoint.

[21] VH, p. 158.
[22] *Ibid.,* pp. 160-61.

Gogarten illustrates this historical view of Christianity with the work of his teacher Ernst Troeltsch. Troeltsch regards Christianity in the context of Western intellectual history as one of many manifestations of the human spirit. Since the historian must make his description of any phenomenon sufficiently encompassing, Troeltsch characterizes Christianity as a synthetic compound of Judaism, Jesus, Paul's mysticism, Plato, Roman law, etc. Two things result from this way of viewing Christianity as a historical phenomenon: 1) the old metaphysical dogma is dead and Jesus becomes a purely human figure, and 2) Christianity is viewed as a way of life which man must achieve apart from the divinely infused power of the sacrament. Gogarten sees the contemporary historical idea of Christianity, therefore, as a secularization of Christianity. In this Christianity the personhood man *receives in faith* has become a form of ethical existence to be achieved by man's own action.[23]

Gogarten points out that the theological revolt of the 1920's (which he helped inaugurate) was a radical assault on this secularized Christianity in the name of authentic Christian faith. Although he still believes that this task of *distinguishing* Christianity and Christian faith is a central one for theology, he finds those who engage in denunciations of the "Christian West" a little like the man who curses the ass on which he is sitting.[24] The only way to treat the secularization of Christianity seriously is to try to regain an understanding of authentic Christian faith itself through a dialogue with the outlook of a radically secularized world which no longer acknowledges the mystery out of which faith lives. The next step, therefore, in tracing Gogarten's effort to understand secularization theologically is to examine his analysis of the modern form of secularization.

[23] *Ibid.,* p. 155.
[24] *Ibid.*

41

3

Secular Man

Gogarten finds the distinguishing characteristic of modern secularity—in contrast to the secularization achieved by the New Testament—in the *negative* sense given to man's independence.[25] The struggle against the church has meant that even the divine mystery is thought of as an enslaving power from which man must be liberated if he is to be truly human. As a result modern autonomous man gropes within himself for his counterpart, and, because he no longer meets a genuine opposite for response, the active, productive side of his nature has undergone a tremendous hypertrophy at the expense of the receptive side. In his most recent work Gogarten has called this hypertrophy "subjectivism." He does not mean by this a failure of objectivity in the sense of letting one's prejudices interfere with research. Subjectivism is not a particular epistemological theory but the horizon within which modern man thinks and acts. In dealing with subjectivism Gogarten has found an ally in Martin Heidegger who characterizes the entire period since Descartes as the era of the subject. It is most characteristic of this "subject-ism," says Heidegger, that it prides itself on its objectivity, since the swing back and forth between subjectivity and objectivity reflects a relation to the world more fundamental than any of the epistemologies of the period. What typifies this relation to beings is the "conquest of the world as a picture." [26] We cannot "let things be" as they present themselves but must grasp, measure, analyze, and represent

[25] German has two words for "independence," which enable Gogarten to make a distinction between a positive independence in which the emphasis is on man's maturity and responsibility for the world, and a negative independence in which the emphasis is on man's refusal of any determination beyond himself. The former is designated *Selbständigkeit* (able to stand by oneself), the latter *Unabhängigkeit* (not dependent on another).

[26] Martin Heidegger, "Die Zeit des Weltbildes," in *Holzwege* (Frankfurt M., 1950), p. 87.

in order to certify the object by standards we have created. As one who represents beings to himself, man has become the *subjectum* who throws himself down as the foundation upon which "all that is in the manner of its being and its truth is grounded." [27]

Gogarten merges Heidegger's analysis with his own concern for secularization to arrive at his definition of subjectivism: "man's independence toward the world understood as a world view." [28] In a world dominated by subjectivism the receptive dimension of man's nature has atrophied to the point that responsibility retains only a moralistic sense. As a result the meanings of "world" and "personhood" which emerged in the original desacralization wrought by Christian faith have been altered. When autonomy is experienced as an absolute, the world is transformed into a neutral field of objects and the person is transmuted into a world-viewing subject. In the original autonomy of man opened up in faith, independence meant the maturity of a son who bore his freedom in the knowledge of his rootedness in the mystery of his life with others in the world. But for the modern experience personhood does not reside in this belonging but in independence conceived as an end in itself. Consequently Gogarten calls this kind of personhood "personality" since it is a task, something to be

[27] *Ibid.* p. 81. At first glance Gogarten's analysis of the fate of Christian responsibility might seem parallel to Heidegger's audacious contention that Western history has been headed ever deeper into forgetfulness of Being since the time of the pre-Socratics. Yet not only has Heidegger explicitly denied that the "oblivion of Being" has anything to do with secularization (Old-Marburger meeting of 1961), but he has indicated repeatedly that belief or unbelief in God simply has no effect on the destiny of Being. The "effect" is the other way around. As Heidegger remarks in *Holzwege,* "Today the reduction of the essence of modernity to the self-evident is accomplished. Once this is assured as a world view the fertile soil will be readied for a primordial interrogation of Being, which will open up the field of decision as to whether Being will once again be capable of a God, whether the essence of the Truth of Being will take the essence of man more orginatively into its claim" (p. 103).

[28] WG, p. 95 (Eng. tr., p. 95).

realized by the continual affirmation and expression of autonomy.[29] In the original responsibility for the world available to man in faith the world was cared for as an inheritance received from God. But for the man who lives under the destiny of subjectivism the world is simply there as a neutral realm over which he rules because he wills to do so.[30]

If it is only a few who have been able to articulate this modern consciousness of aseity, Gogarten sees it nevertheless as the archimedean point of our secularized culture. But one should not think the ethos of freedom which Gogarten describes is merely a humorless dedication to duty or a kind of pessimism of the strong—it may assume the sunny metaphors of Nietzsche's Zarathustra. And yet even the heroic yea-sayer's dance of life is finally a dance with himself. For at the root of the modern ethos Gogarten finds nothing but

the naked, bare responsibility of man for the world. This responsibility is naked and bare because in it man depends wholly on himself and on what only he can do. Perhaps man has never been so lonely in his world, so dependent upon himself . . . as he is in this responsibility. Wherever modern man may turn, in all that he encounters, he encounters himself.[31]

But this experience of aseity, Gogarten contends, is an optical illusion brought about by man's having turned from the divine mystery and got himself tied in a contorted knot of self-reflection. A heavy necessity forces man into this introversion since the sacral powers have been fully depotentiated by Christian faith, so that once he has turned from God there is no power in the world before which he can be responsible—except

---

[29] "Before God I am not a personality (*Persönlichkeit*) but a person (*Person*). It is striking that I cannot say of myself: I am a personality. By contrast I can very well say that I am a person before God." (MZGW, p. 130.)

[30] *Ibid.*, p. 186.

[31] WG, p. 190 (Eng. tr., p. 187).

himself.[32] Gogarten goes so far as to compare this self-grounded responsibility with the "service of cosmic powers" of which Paul speaks in Galatians. Modern man's responsibility no longer has the merely proximate sense of caring for the immediate future while receiving the wholeness of the world and himself from God, but now his responsibility is aimed at securing the ultimate destiny of the world. Gogarten finds the guiding principle of this effort to guarantee the order and wholeness of the world through the works of responsibility in the idea of perfecting the world. But since man has become *a se* by robbing God of his aseity, this drive for perfection knows no boundary or limit to human action, so that even persons may be sacrificed to the goal of progress. Gogarten does not view the perilous tendency of our technological societies toward herd behavior as a contradiction of the experience of aseity but as its confirmation. For the dissolution of the organic bonds of familial and communal life under the relentless extension of secularization has pushed men who seek a bond beyond themselves into the hands of the political and social "leaders" who serve up an ideological cement for human life through the medium of racial, religious, or national mythology. The difference between the present situation of Christian faith and that of the early church is that the early Christian sought freedom from bondage to the cosmic powers, whereas the modern Christian who is free of the world seeks a bond which can give coherence to his life without derogating his independence.[33]

The answer to the ideological temptation, Gogarten believes, is neither pious exhortations to maintain one's freedom and independence nor is it the promulgation of some form of "Christian" or "natural" law which will serve to bind man from above. Once the world is secularized we can permit neither church nor state to set the fundamental boundaries of life but

[32] MZGW, pp. 166-67.
[33] VJC, pp. 458-66.

45

only the individual human conscience. And yet how can the man who is responsible for himself and stands as the final arbiter of what he is and believes find a genuine counterpart to whom he may be bound without surrendering his independence and freedom? Or if he does remain the independent master of himself and the world, can he acknowledge a counterpart outside himself without making this bond depend on his own subjective chóice? It appears almost as though an acoustical illusion has now set in; even if one were to hear the voice of God he would take it for the voice of his own conscience. Here in the inescapable subjectivity of modern existence Gogarten finds the cutting edge of the problem secularization puts to theology.

There are several questions about Gogarten's analysis of secularization which need to be raised at this point. To begin with there are difficulties in his notion that Christian faith is the origin of modern secularization and historicization in some sort of causal sense. First of all the category of a pre-Christian man who lives in unity with the cosmos is so broad that he has already had to exclude Judaism and the Greeks and in fact should have excluded certain aspects of Buddhism, too. Secondly, Gogarten obviously elevates one aspect of Pauline thought to the status of a canon within the canon. Moreover he admits that even Paul did not carry out the full implications of mature sonship in regard to responsibility for the world—that was left for Luther. One cannot help but suspect that the presence in the New Testament of a Judaic dualism of an earthly and heavenly world and the obvious tendency to treat Christ as a new lawgiver are as responsible for the early Christians' failure to develop the independence of man from the world as was the baneful influence of Hellenism.

Even more problematic is Gogarten's explanation of why the secularization of the world in Christian faith did not take effect for fifteen hundred years. He paints the amazing spectacle of secularization springing into the world with Jesus, only to plunge underground whence after fifteen hundred years it was summoned up by Luther, only to be driven immediately back underground by Orthodoxy, until definitively liberated by the philosophers of the Enlightenment who forbade it to appear henceforth in its original Christian form. The picture would be a lot more convincing if we had been shown there were always powerful forces in the church which championed the independence of man. To blame Hellenistic philosophy for the perversion of the New Testament faith is hardly an adequate explanation of so fantastic an about-face on the issue of man's maturity as Gogarten finds in the period between Paul and Luther. His strictures against the Middle Ages seem particularly tendentious, and he ignores the many instances outside monastic reformers and the mystics who championed the independence of human reason in general and the "secular arm" in particular. Ironically this depreciation of the power of resistance to the forces which tended to make the Medieval Church a cosmically grounded hierarchy enclosing man's freedom makes Luther the hero at the expense of seriously weakening the case for the Christian origin of secularization. But even if Gogarten had taken the trouble to show a continuity between the secularization inaugurated by the New Testament and certain aspects of medieval thought and culture, the fact remains that most of those from the Renaissance on who struck off the shackles of the church did not appeal to Christian precedent, but where they did appeal to the past it was to the classical models—to the very people Gogarten believes were not sufficiently liberated from the encompassing cosmos.

If we turn next to Gogarten's characterization of modern man, we again feel ill at ease with some of the broad generalizations which guide his analysis. Although there is much in Heidegger's notion of "subject-ism" which rings true, the implication that all modern philosophies or revivals are under its sway would require an extensive justification to achieve more status than that of an oracular pronouncement. But this objection does not detract from Gogarten's basic contention that theology must henceforth be pursued in the context of human freedom and independence. Perhaps the least convincing element in his analysis of modern secularity, however, is his argument that once the world has lost its sacral character, the man who refuses the divine counterpart inevitably puts himself in the place of God. No doubt this has often happened, but there are many in the Western world who recognize full well that the perfectionist drive leads to "playing God" with one's fellowmen, and they do their best to remain genuinely secular and simply leave a void where the old God of Christendom once reigned. Gogarten's description of the contemporary situation is always at its best in the passages where he acknowledges the courage and perseverance of those outside of faith who strive to remain genuinely secular.

Although it is hard to accept as *historically* accurate Gogarten's contention that Christian faith stands in a causal relationship to secularization, his *theological* argument that faith is not only compatible with secularization but demands its continuance, remains intact. If he is right theologically, then the effort to turn secularization back and escape the radical implications of the historicizing of human existence would be a movement against faith itself. Such an attempt would in effect surrender the freedom of faith for the servitude of an outmoded Christian world view. The fundamental implication of Gogarten's position, therefore, is that secularization is a one-way street. Accordingly, the only path theology can seriously follow is to enter into a dialogue with the "subject-ist" presuppositions of the secular mode of existence in an effort to regain an understanding of a faith that can hold together both the active and receptive dimensions of man's existence in their integrity. Since the desacralization of the cosmos by faith also meant that the man of faith henceforth experienced the world as history, Gogarten's opening gambit in the dialogue with subjectivism is to discover where the imprint of the *question* of faith in God is to be found in man's experience of the historicity of his existence. The most far-reaching effect of Christian faith on human life—embracing both believer and unbeliever—is the historicizing of human existence which has accompanied secularization.[34]

---

[34] VH, p. 106.

II

HISTORICITY AND THE
HIDDENNESS OF GOD

1

The Question

Our dilemma as secular men in an era dominated by
the subject-object dialectic is not how we can still believe there
is a god, but whether it is possible for our god to be God the
Creator and Redeemer. It is a commonplace not only of contemporary theology but of most of the Jewish-Christian tradition that God cannot be an object we represent to ourselves and
certify as real without his ceasing to be God for us. Yet modern
self-consciousness can only recognize as real something for
which man can take over responsibility. Or as Nietzsche put

it: "God is a conjecture; but I desire that your conjectures should be limited by what is thinkable. Could you *think* a god?" The dilemma into which we are thrown by the collision between biblical faith and modern self-consciousness can be expressed by paraphrasing Archibald MacLeish, "If God is real he is not God, if God is God he is not real. Take the even take the odd." The "even" choice, of course, is to capitulate and admit that God is not real (or that language about him is nonsense), but to assert that nevertheless belief in a God serves some useful function, that the word "God" stands for a set of values we have projected, an orientation to the world, a readiness to behave in a certain way. The "odd" choice for theology is to accept the primacy of the subject as the inevitable concomitant of man's maturity and yet uncover the point at which the claim of aseity is vulnerable to its own temporality.

Although it may seem that in making the "odd" choice Gogarten is granting an uncommonly large place in theology to a passing phase of Western thought, he suggests that unless we want to end up with a "thing" god, the question of God cannot be asked apart from the pressure of man's quest for his own humanity in the present historical moment.[1] Gogarten's point is simply that if God is in fact the Creator, then we stand even now in his power. Since self-grounded freedom and autonomy are the unquestioned presuppositions of modernity, theology will serve the Christian community by reminding it that God deals with man precisely in this experience of freedom and autonomy and not in some kind of religious or supernatural realm. So long as Christians are alive to the historicity of God they will not take the message of the New Testament as a substitute for autonomous responsibility, but as its fulfillment. Or, in more formal terms, Gogarten is concerned that the message

[1] Friedrich Gogarten, "Entscheidung im Nichts," *Eckart*, 1952, p. 294.

51

not be misconstrued as an ideological edition of the law but allowed to be the gospel which both sharpens and at the same time fulfills the demand of autonomy.

If we are to see Gogarten's concern with the hiddenness of God in its proper context, we need to look more closely at the law-gospel theme which has been a basic model for his theological reflection.[2] The key to Gogarten's view of the law-gospel pattern is the distinction he makes between two uses of the law. First, he describes the law as the counterpart of the gospel within the Word of God. If we recall that "Word of God" for Gogarten is analogous to the immediate word of personal relation in which another makes himself present for me, then the Word of God must be understood as the prevenient presence of the divine mystery which is both gift (gospel) and demand (law). The Word of God is law in the same way another person's promise demands my faith in him simply by virtue of his having pledged himself in his word. Thus law and gospel in this first sense always go together and one is not before the other, as though the gift of presence could be bestowed without giving rise to the demand to receive it, or as though the demand to receive it could be made a criterion for the bestowal of the gift.[3] For Gogarten, then, the only way to fulfill the law which makes this single demand is to believe in the gospel, i.e., to receive the gift by surrendering oneself to the divine mystery. It should be evident that he considers the law in this form not as something commanded by the divine mystery but as the mystery itself, or, in Luther's terms, that we are not dealing here with the commands but the Commander.[4]

The other use of the law is made up from the commands

---

[2] Gogarten's most comprehensive and systematic postwar work, *Der Mensch zwischen Gott und Welt*, is devoted entirely to a treatment of the problem of secularization in terms of the law-gospel framework.

[3] *Ibid.*, pp. 26-28.

[4] *Ibid.*, p. 35.

which, for Gogarten, are the historical demands and obligations we discover and shape in giving order to our world.[5] The crux of the law-gospel problem for his thought is obviously the relation between the law in its concrete form of many historical demands and the law which accompanies the gospel as its single demand. Gogarten believes the highest task of theology is to safeguard 1) the knowledge that it is the *same* mystery which meets me in both "uses" of the law, and 2) the knowledge that the law as the single demand which can only be fulfilled in receptivity to the divine mystery must constantly be *distinguished,* although not separated, from the law as it takes the form of a multitude of demands man can fulfill through his action. Gogarten expresses the togetherness of the two forms of the law by saying that the single demand which can only be fulfilled with one's person (the traditional *verus usus*) is always experienced in the many demands and obligations of our daily life (the traditional *usus politicus*). In other words, a man's response to the unique exigency of the law is not only a matter of responding to the mystery of existence but at the same time a matter of remaining responsible for the daily coherence of the world.[6] It follows that whenever the powerful exigency of the single demand of the oncoming future is experienced in connection with the demands of our daily life, the complex of

[5] This is the most controversial aspect of Gogarten's position on law and gospel, particularly in the form in which he applied it to the political crisis of 1933 in Germany. Stated briefly, he is saying that the Old Testament commandments and the New Testament admonitions are not the law of God for us, but that God's single demand of man's total obedience meets us through the laws of our particular historical-political position, even though it is not identical with them. His position is stated with particular clarity in "Offenbarung und Geschichte" *Deutsche Theologie,* 1935, pp. 115-31; "Die Lehre von den zwei Reichen und das 'natürliche Gesetz'" *Deutsche Theologie,* 1935, pp. 331-40; and "Wort Gottes und Schrift" *Deutsche Theologie,* 1936, pp. 197-219. One should also consult the better known pamphlets from the early days of the Church Struggle: *Einheit von Evangelium und Volkstum?* (1933), and *Ist Volksgesetz Gottesgesetz?* (1934).

[6] MZGW, pp. 102-5, 209-10, 215-16.

customary moral scruples and ideological securities is banished from consciousness, and the naked, hard core of the First Commandment stands forth in everything. In this experience of total impotence before the mysterious ground of responsibility a man stands under the pressure of the *deus absconditus,* the hidden God. Once this happens a man perceives his contingency and lostness in such a way that he is ripe for being opened to the *knowledge* of the divine mystery in Jesus (gospel).[7]

Since the law of the world in its particular historical form always presents itself as the final presupposition and goal which man must fulfill if he is to give himself and his world meaning and permanence, part of theology's task is to discover where the unquestioned presuppositions of the modern self-understanding become questionable. Of course, God might use anything to drive a man to his senses, but Gogarten points out that whatever the particular occasion—be it the flip of a cigarette or falling sleet—it is only a divine work where *man himself* is brought to bay and not merely some part of him, where man not only inquires about things but is interrogated in his possibility of being. But how can that happen today, Gogarten asks, when it is a self-evident truth that the fundamental order of our world is the mechanistic-causal one uncovered by the physical sciences and spread into every aspect of life through technology? In accordance with this ground plan we are developing specialists for every area of research, but when we come to ask about man and the world as a whole, there is no science for it, since the whole cannot be reduced to an object area of investigation. In the subjectist schema of reality, whatever its particular epistemological form, man can only come into question under specified aspects available to research.[8]

Thus the sway of subjectivism excludes anything like genuine

---

[7] Gogarten, "Wort Gottes und Schrift," *Deutsche Theologie,* 1936, pp. 209-11.

[8] Gogarten, "Entscheidung im Nichts," *Eckart,* 1952, p. 293.

mystery, i.e., a question whose answer involves the being of the one who questions. Genuine mystery in Gogarten's definition is a power before which man's thought recoils in the awareness that his thought and existence already "belong" in it.[9] Gogarten believes that if man is to remain human, he must perceive the question of his humanity as a question in which he always stands and from which he can never escape. Then, Gogarten remarks, he may realize that he is not only asking but being asked, that this questioning corresponds to a hidden origin and end.[10]

Gogarten's definition of mystery is obviously parallel to Marcel's distinction between mystery and problem, but the resonance which comes from the preoccupation with the concept of nothingness reflects not only the influence of Luther but also of Heidegger. As Heidegger suggested in his "notorious" address, "What is Metaphysics?" in a time when only beings count or, as we are accustomed to say, when only things matter—Being is reduced to the status of nothing.[11] One is even tempted to say that things themselves are more and more fraught with nothing, wearing out sooner to be replaced with new models or editions, so that we increasingly become caretakers of our own obsolescence. When we inquire into the being of man we come finally not only to a point where we do not yet know anything, but to a point where we can in principle know nothing through the mode of objectifying thought. But, to recall Nietzsche, what we cannot think we must not think or, if one prefers Wittgenstein, whereof one cannot speak thereof one must be silent. Gogarten is saying that our aseity as modern men forbids us to admit the reality of a phenomenon which is not a thing available to the certification of a subject.

[9] MZGW, pp. 341-42.
[10] Gogarten, "Entscheidung im Nichts," *Eckart,* 1952, p. 293.
[11] Martin Heidegger, *Was ist Metaphysik?* (1929).

But there is a deeper level of meaning to Gogarten's concept of mystery than the simple notion of a phenomenon which cannot be reduced to an objectified thing. For to encounter a power which is not subject to human manipulation obviously threatens the experience of aseity which lies at the heart of modern self-awareness. In one sense, for man to acknowledge the reality of his involvement in mystery is to admit the nothingness of himself when he tries to be the basis of all being and meaning. Yet Gogarten does not conceive this experience of mystery solely as a matter of existential anxiety or guilt. Rather the mystery which surrounds and penetrates human life in the world is experienced not only by those who become guilty, or aware of their being toward death, but by everyone who trusts, or loves, or forgives. But these experiences only reveal genuine mystery to us when they occur in their fundamental sense, i.e., where our being or nonbeing is at stake. Thus genuine trust does not occur where I am confident of somebody because I have reason to believe he will keep his promise, but where I trust him without reserve, exposing myself to all the risks involved. This is a trust that makes no calculations or guesses, but trusts where there is nothing to trust. Nor is its trusting beyond the limits of the socially and politically calculable, a matter of resignation or despair, but a letting-go of all security and remaining-open to the mysterious power of human obligation.[12]

All these ways of experiencing mystery reach their sharpest expression at the point of the historical ethos or law which cements life together. This is true in the highest degree for modern man whose law is his self-grounded freedom and responsibility. But just as this responsibility is the privileged place where the mystery will break into consciousness, it is also the chief means of suppressing any awareness of the riddle of

[12] Gogarten, "Entscheidung im Nichts," *Eckart,* 1952, pp. 297-98.

existence. For by their responsibility men create the forms of life and thought which make human community possible—the customs, goals, institutions, interpretations which secure the world against the threat of chaos and meaninglessness. Of course any failure of this responsibility or even the euphoria of an astonishing success—one thinks of the Bomb—may open a man's mind anew to the question of the source and ground of responsibility.[13]

But wherever responsibility *is* accompanied by the question of the meaning of existence as a whole, man is directed to the mystery of himself and the world. For a responsibility which touches him in his essence as person demands a counterpart to which he can respond. To become aware that his humanity is not simply given but something to be decided, is to let himself be sensitized for the mysteriousness of his being in the world. Gogarten calls this awareness of the questionableness of existence a directedness toward the mystery of man's humanity in the world. What a man knows "in this not-knowing" is a "mysterious revealing power to which his directedness points." [14]

According to Gogarten, then, the place where the question of God becomes real and urgent for man today—whether or not he consciously thinks of the question as directing him to "god"—is the ethos of autonomy and responsibility which gives modern existence its historical character. Gogarten considers two elements essential if man is to experience the world historically: first, he must be responsible for himself and the order of the world, and second, he must never resolve or abandon the question of the meaning of history as a whole. In terms of the present discussion of mystery, this means that genuine history is only possible where man's responsibility for the world, especially as expressed in science and technology, is anchored in his directedness to the mystery of the world. It

[13] MZGW, p. 216.
[14] *Ibid.*, p. 379.

follows that man's existence does not remain automatically historical; genuine historicity is something he can fail to maintain. Ordinarily we think of nothing more given than history, since the stream of events seems to grind relentlessly on, no matter how we exercise our responsibility. But such an automatic constancy would not be history at all in Gogarten's view, but simply a natural process. Therefore, before we can go on to a discussion of the way the question of God and the question of history mutually involve each other, we need to take a closer look at Gogarten's understanding of historical reality.

2

History

Although Gogarten believes that the concept of historical reality, implicit in many contemporary theories of historical explanation, is a special case of the absence of the question of man from technologically oriented thought, the very failure of the discipline of history to establish itself as a science points to a greater awareness that man himself, and not just his functions is the subject of history. This is also seen in the continuing debate over the objectivity of written history and perhaps clearest of all in the state of the two traditional approaches to history—documentary research and the synthetic philosophy of history. As Gogarten points out, historical research piles up evidence trying to find out what has *happened:* Did the event reported by the generally received witnesses actually take place, and did it happen the way they reported it? The synthetic philosophy of history, on the other hand, begins with the question, *What* happened; given the events reported by research, what is the meaning of events? [15] Both need each other

[15] VH, p. 110. The philosophy of history meant here is called "synthetic," in the sense of synthesis as opposed to the "critical" philosophy of history which deals with epistemological questions. Cf. W. H. Walsh, *Philosophy of History: An Introduction* (New York, 1960), pp. 9-10. Gogarten's own

since research does not know what to look for, nor can it present its results, without a certain context of meaning, and the synthetic philosophy of history in seeking *the* meaning of history must always use the results of research. Historical research has been able to go on its way relatively undisturbed, but the synthetic philosophy of history has been rendered almost impossible by the fact that all systems of meaning, including Christianity, are recognized as historical and thus not valid for the whole of history. The philosophy of history has two possibilities in this situation. One is to accept the relativity of all historical phenomena and renounce the question of the unity and meaning of history; the other is to seek the meaning in some kind of transcendence. Either way is to give up the question of man. No matter how ingenious or energetic the philosopher, he can never arrive at the meaning of history by adding up the results of research, since he would have to wait until history were at an end. On the other hand, to find the meaning of history by an appeal to the transcendental or super-historical obviously turns to a realm above history and is thus no longer the meaning of *history*. Gogarten is led to conclude that the two approaches by which modern historical thought has tried to conceive of history "are such that on the one hand historical research does not reach history at all and on the other hand the [synthetic] philosophy of history reaches far beyond it." [16]

At the root of this dilemma of either surrendering the question of man in relativism or prematurely settling it by appeal to a transcendent meaning, Gogarten finds what we may call the inherited preconception of the historical field which dominates modern research. Preconception does not mean a bias in the

---

analysis is concerned with both the theological counterpart of the "critical" philosophy of history, and with what one could call the "ontology" of history, the attempt to delineate the region of reality which gives rise to the subject matter of what we call history.

[16] VH, p. 121.

usual sense, but the implicit conception of what history is that opens up the area of research as such. Without an implicit notion of the nature of historical reality and historical narrative, we could never go about either research or synthesis, we could not even "let the facts speak for themselves" since we can only dis-cover them on the basis of our notion of what a fact is. The chief preconception operating in research, which affects the possibility of our asking the question of man, is the idea of a historical construction: the historian's task is to create self-explanatory unities out of the deposit of the past. Each narrative is to be an interconnected whole, whether it be the history of a nation, a revolution, or the development of an art style, and this whole is to be forged in terms of the causal interplay of personal, social, economic, and political forces.[17]

Insofar as history is known it is closed; events which at the moment of occurrence were sheer becoming are now frozen and stand as monuments to the human spirit. Of course the constructions may be revised in the light of new data, but the fact remains that the ideal is a self-explanatory and enclosed construction. As all the sciences have become more and more specialized, historical reality has been treated solely in terms of the various individual constructions produced by research, and even the synthetic philosophy of history tries to take these separate histories and weave them into a self-explanatory whole. Both research and synthesis are alike in this respect: they view history from the perspective of the self-contained subject. What is aimed at here, Gogarten asserts, is "a spectator's attitude to history, in which the spectator holds himself aloof from history, or is under obligation to

[17] *Ibid.*, pp. 115-22. Behind Gogarten's analysis here is Ernst Troeltsch's concept of historical "individualities" (cf. *Ibid.*, p. 122). One will find a similar characterization of historical conceptuality in Raymond Aron's essay, "De l'objet de l'histoire," especially in the section on "Les unités historiques" (Aron, *Dimensions de la conscience historiques;* Paris, 1961), pp. 95 ff.

hold himself as aloof as he can." [18] And this basic subject-object structure is unchanged even if the historian attempts a sympathetic understanding or chooses models from the drama; it is still the look or empathy of the experiencing subject that predominates in an effort to construct a narrative which is self-contained. Man in his historicity never becomes the direct intention of the questions asked by the historian under these presuppositions since the investigator is forbidden by his conception of historical construction to raise the question of the meaning of the whole; and the philosopher of history in his effort to synthesize the constructions dissolves the *question* of man, since any principle by which he seeks to synthesize would foreclose on the future by treating history as though it were at an end.[19]

The point of Gogarten's analysis is not to suggest that historical research is wrong in its preoccupation with increasingly limited constructions aimed at specialized questions, but to illuminate the fact that historical reality, as it is concretely experienced, is far from being fully embraced in this preconceptual scheme. Therefore, if theology is to do justice to the question of man in history it cannot simply take over a view of history from which this question is excluded *a priori*. In his own effort to develop an understanding of historical reality appropriate to the human question of God, Gogarten's work has gone through two stages. The first grew out of his early critique of Ernst Troeltsch's historicism and received its definitive formulation in *I Believe in the Triune God* (1926).[20] His basic theme there was that history cannot be understood from the perspective of the isolated self since the stuff of historical reality is interpersonal encounter under the conditions of temporality. If we start from the subject, the "I" which is

[18] EK, p. 36 (Eng. tr., p. 27).
[19] VH, p. 120.
[20] Friedrich Gogarten, *Ich glaube an den dreieinigen Gott*, p. 60.

above history, the only question can be, how are the encounters of men to be explained? But if history is approached from *within* the relation to others, the question cannot be whether we can explain others but whether we are open to their presence and claim as persons.[21] It is important to notice, however, that Gogarten does not derive his concept of historical reality as interpersonal encounter from a general I-Thou philosophy, but from his understanding of Creation. Belief in God the Creator is not knowledge about the origin of the world but the acknowledgment of God as Creator of the concrete situation in which man now stands. And the principle content of this concrete situation, according to the Bible, is the actual relationship with other men. Thus Creation is drawn into the Thou-I relation since

there is no faith which, in believing in God, does not at the same time believe in the other man, the Thou—the Bible says: the neighbor—through whom God speaks with us and to whom we are thereby indissolubly bound.[22]

When seen in this light, faith in Creation becomes "the constitutive element in history." [23]

Does this emphasis on actual relationships not eliminate the past as genuine history? On the contrary, Gogarten contends that the emphasis on encounter lets the past be genuinely past, since his understanding of historical reality does not dissolve the otherness of the past in an explanation or interpretation. "For only when a Thou meets me in something past and when I am thus called by this past to a decision, can this past be history." [24] The genuine dialectic of history from a theological point of view, therefore, is not between history and superhistory

[21] *Ibid.*, pp. 59-60.
[22] *Ibid.*, p. 60. For a comparison of Gogarten's "Thou-I" with Buber's "I-Thou/I-it" polarity see the Appendix, pp. 199-200.
[23] *Ibid.*, p. 65.
[24] *Ibid.*, p. 73.

or even between the relative and the absolute, but the completely temporal dialectic within history between past and present, visible and invisible. To believe in Creation, for example, is to believe that history is the work of God, yet it is not visibly his work since what is visible is only human will and action.[25]

Gogarten draws two further implications from this interpersonal understanding of historical reality. First, not every event in the past is history, i.e., has the power to be present historically, but only those events which encounter us as a past Thou and call for a decision. This applies, of course, not only to individual persons but also to communities such as Israel. Second, and more important, *we* do not choose what events of the past and present will be history for us, but the events themselves lay claim on us through present witnesses to the tradition which these events have sustained.

Not what I call out of the past is history . . . history is something past which calls me to a present decision . . . which encounters me as a present Thou and claims me and through this claim inseparably binds me to itself.[26]

Thus the interpersonal character of history means that the past can never be absorbed into the present, but can be present only as the past, since it is not a past in general but the concrete claim of other persons. When a past Thou is made present by an explanation or theory, the past is in effect absorbed into the present, it becomes an object to be represented and contemplated rather than a question and claim on my person, in short, it ceases to happen.

Gogarten's purpose in developing this understanding of history was to enable us to approach the "Christian event" on its own terms rather than subjecting it to modern categories; more particularly his purpose was to show how "Jesus himself

[25] *Ibid.*, pp. 79-80.
[26] *Ibid.*, p. 83.

can be present in his own historical reality and not only in an explanation." [27] To follow Gogarten's application of his interpersonal concept of historical reality to Israel, Jesus, and the church, would carry us beyond our present concern. This much should be indicated, however: Gogarten climaxes his work by showing that since the full hearing and receiving of the neighbor has taken place in Jesus, his word alone has the power to overcome our isolation by opening us to God and the neighbor.[28] And since human life is fully historical only when it is lived in acknowledgment of the claim of others, only through hearing and living from the claim of the life of Jesus is a genuinely historical existence possible. Thus if the word of Jesus spoken to me through the word of a present Thou overcomes my claim to be the center of life and meaning, then I am bound to Jesus and in him to God and my neighbor. In this sense Gogarten can conclude in *I Believe in the Triune God,* that the church's announcement of God's coming to us in Jesus is not only a reference to something historical, but actually creates history.[29]

Two things are particularly important in Gogarten's understanding of history in terms of the Thou-I relation. First the locus of historical reality is not in the configuration of forces, or in the movement of the largest numbers, but in the ordinary encounters of everyday life. The question of whether these encounters are really historical is whether there is actually an encounter or only the assertion of the subject, the I as it endeavors to remain in control of its world. When this perspective is applied to the past, it means that the prime question of history for man is not the reliability of a reported sequence of happenings but the claim of certain men and events of the past to be the dialogical partners of my present existence.

[27] *Ibid.,* p. 130.
[28] *Ibid.,* pp. 158-59.
[29] *Ibid.,* pp. 163-64, 180-81.

The second thing which emerges in Gogarten's understanding of history in this period is his way of locating the claim of God the Creator in the claim of the other man, both past and present. Translated into Gogarten's later terminology, this means the question of God becomes urgent where the question of my humanity is at stake in my encounter with other men. The very presence of another man is a claim on me to be *there* for him, to be present with myself, but I can only genuinely be there for him if I am open to him in such a way that I in fact receive my being from him. In other words, genuine history only occurs where a man is open to the mystery which meets him in the trust or betrayal, forgiveness or guilt he experiences in relation to others.

With his Thou-I interpretation of history developed between 1921 and 1926, Gogarten launched the first large-scale theological critique of subjectivism. But by the 1930's, the I-Thou motif, especially in Buber's form, was becoming so overworked as to lose much of its suggestive power, and Gogarten turned increasingly to the concept of responsibility through which he sought to convey the same basic meaning. The responsibility motif, however, permitted him to broaden his understanding of history by pointing up the social-political dimension of encounter, and, in an incidental way, also helped him to avoid the personalistic sentimentality which can so easily creep into I-Thou discussion. After 1948, when the problem of secularization began to hold the center of his theological concerns, "responsibility" proved even more useful since it carried a strong sense of active self-determination. Thus in his later work Gogarten finds in responsibility the "constitutive element of history," since there can only be what we call history where "the world no longer encompasses man, but where man has taken over responsibility for it." [30]

---

[30] Friedrich Gogarten, "Zur Frage nach dem Ursprung des geschichtlichen Denkens," *Evangelische Theologie*, 1954, p. 229.

The Secularization of History

Here again we must keep in mind that Gogarten is concerned with concrete historical actuality and not merely with those events which are considered worthy of memory because of their quantitative institutional or intellectual impact on later generations. Gogarten bases his evaluation of the most ordinary and personal aspects of existence on the way the biblical saga treats history. The point at which the biblical narrative is most unlike the historical constructions of the modern period is not so much the factor of supernatural intervention as the density or mysterious depth of the biblical story.[31] Neither the inner life of the spirit nor a configuration of forces constitutes the fabric of history for the biblical writers, but what happens in the everyday decisions and actions of ordinary people, in such completely human events as the strife of two brothers, the dream of young Jacob, the escape of a few thousand slaves from Egypt, the preaching of Jesus. The density of these events is their complete historicity, their humanly "unexpected, unpredictable occurrence and this in the sense of an accident." [32] Unlike both Greek and modern historical narrative in which everything is in the foreground and accounted for, the biblical saga is never well rounded but always filled with "paratactic gaps." In this absence of a surface coherence and completeness the biblical narrative is closer to the realism of those modern novelists who refuse the standpoint of omniscience.[33] The biblical writers tell their story from the perspective of those who are immersed in history, for whom what happened and is about to happen comes from the unfathomable mystery of the divine will. Thus the density of biblical narrative derives from the opaqueness of the future. According to Gogarten, it is this impenetrability of the mystery-laden future

[31] ZThK, 1954, p. 328.
[32] *Ibid.,* p. 324.
[33] *Ibid.,* pp. 325 and 329.

hanging over all decisions and happenings which makes them genuinely historical.

The prominence of the future in Gogarten's later work on faith and history demands further comment since it is the key to his understanding of the hiddenness of God in history. Whereas the prime temporal concern of his Thou-I period is the dialectic of past and present in terms of encounter, now the future takes precedence—not that the past has been eliminated but that the past is known in the present from a posture of openness to the future. For genuine responsibility is only possible where the future is not decided in advance; history simply ceases to be historical if the future is not open. Gogarten derives this notion from New Testament eschatology which he interprets as signifying not only a chronological end, but primarily the end of the world's religious power to enclose the life of man. But this end is also a beginning, a new relation to the world in which man remains open for what comes.[34] Or to put it another way, the biblical God never appears in his full presence as do the Homeric gods, only "something" of him appears, his hand, his backside. This "ungraspableness" is not accidental but the peculiar way in which God chooses to appear—always as the Coming One who can never be grasped in his full presence by man. By the "density" of biblical history Gogarten means its eschatological character, its occurring out of an impenetrable and undeterminable future. This understanding of historical reality runs counter to the modern concept of history as a series of self-explanatory and enclosed units created out of the past, since the concept of historical reality which corresponds to this view of the past treats the future as something to be mastered and anticipated on the basis of past and present.[35] Gogarten finds a certain irony in the fact that it was historical research which redis-

[34] VH, p. 177.
[35] *Ibid.*, p. 181.

covered New Testament eschatology and with it the particular history and historicity of the New Testament understanding of revelation. For if the

end and beginning which are set for men by the on-coming future of God . . . put him before the question of whether and how he can endure it, and if this question is . . . the question of himself . . . then it is the question in which his history meets him and by which he is called into this history.[36]

The eschatological character of history, therefore, is the ever coming future of the Judgment which, although it remains totally beyond our control, is nevertheless always present in its imminence, setting an end to a life lived out of the world, and the beginning of a life lived out of the future of God. Roger Mehl succinctly expressed what Gogarten is driving at here when he wrote: "Eschatology preserves the historicity of history." [37]

When Gogarten speaks of the future as oncoming he is taking advantage of the German *Zukunft* (from *zu-kommen*) to emphasize that this future is something "always arriving" rather than something "not yet arrived." If we think of the future in terms of our plans for the next few days or months or even of happenings that we expect several years from now, we are waiting for a definite event to arrive.[38] Gogarten sets this proximate future which can be more or less anticipated through human foresight and planning over against what he calls the "pure" future which is filled with oncoming possibilities of existence about which we have no knowledge. Where the future is viewed as part of a time line not yet arrived, men

[36] *Ibid.*, p. 180.
[37] Roger Mehl, "Histoire et eschatologie," in *L'homme et l'histoire* (Paris, 1952), p. 319.
[38] VH, p. 178.

deal with it on the basis of the past, and it becomes in one sense a projection of the past. But when the future is awaited as oncoming and impenetrable, men live in expectation since they have no idea what the dark and incalculable imminence will bring. In the presence of this approaching future with its finally undeterminable demands our planning and projecting on the basis of the past can never erase the possibility that all our plans and hopes may come to nothing. This pure future of Gogarten's, then, is the historical expression of the absolute mystery—but here it is an unknown destiny reaching out toward us, clinging preveniently to all our works.[39]

Gogarten does not distinguish these two dimensions of the future with the intent of asking us to choose between them, but to point up the two orientations which are necessary if man's existence is to remain historical. Naturally a man must anticipate the future through his technological and political planning, but the question is whether he will at the same time remain open to the final impenetrability of the future. As Gogarten sees it, history is preserved where men expose themselves to the opaqueness of the future in the humility of their directedness to the mystery and thereby permit their established identity and anticipatory planning to remain in jeopardy. Gogarten sums up the "two moments" which constitute history in this way:

The one is that man takes over responsibility for his life, for its form and development, and for the form of the world. And the other moment is that this responsibility is determined . . . by the knowledge of the wholeness (*das Ganze*) of both man and the world. We could say, a knowledge of the wholeness in the mode of questioning: this responsibility knows questioningly of this wholeness. Today we like to designate this wholeness as the meaning of life and the world. Thus the responsibility which is the second constitutive moment of history quests for meaning. And so long

[39] MZGW, p. 389.

as it remains historical this responsibility can neither get away from this questioning nor get beyond it.[40]

Before going on to consider explicitly the hiddenness of God, a further comment should be made on the shift in Gogarten's view of history. His Thou-I approach to historical reality and the historical character of faith drew criticism from two directions. On the one side Barth and Bonhoeffer asked if there was, in the last analysis, any difference between God and the neighbor for Gogarten.[41] From the other side Bultmann suggested that Gogarten had approached the problem in the right way, but that his work lacked the kind of conceptual clarity which could come from Heidegger's ontological analysis of historicity.[42] The lack of clarity in Gogarten's work, according to Bultmann, stems from Gogarten's having mixed an ontological analysis of historicity in terms of encounter, with the ontic assertion that history only occurs where the I hears and receives the claim of the Thou through Jesus Christ.[43] Bultmann's point is that theology always depends on a pre-theological understanding of man for the clarification of its concepts and therefore must either seek these concepts from philosophy or engage in philosophy itself.[44] Revelation does not give us any new ontological information but is the becoming actual of a new life through Christ. Theology's task, therefore,

[40] VH, pp. 104-5.

[41] Karl Barth, *Theologische Fragen und Antworten* (Zollikon, 1957), p. 141; Dietrich Bonhoeffer, *Akt und Sein* (München, 1956), p. 65 (Eng. tr., pp. 87-88).

[42] Bultmann, *Existence and Faith*, pp. 92-110. The actual purpose of the essay was to defend Bultmann's own theological method, and he uses Gogarten to show that despite the apparent opposition between Gogarten's concept of history as encounter and Heidegger's concept of historicity in terms of resolution in the face of man's unique possibility of coming to an end (death), the former is actually concerned with making an ontic claim which can be best explicated conceptually on the basis of Heidegger's ontological categories.

[43] *Ibid.*, p. 105.

[44] *Ibid.*, p. 98.

is to offer a "conceptual explication of such speaking about the event of revelation, to the end that the man of faith will have a critical knowledge of himself and that preaching will actually speak of revelation and faith." [45] There is a good deal in Gogarten's postwar work which would indicate that he has finally accepted Bultmann's critique. Not only does his concept of history reflect Heidegger's influence, but Gogarten also specifically endorses Heidegger's philosophy in *Demythologizing and History*. There he says of Heidegger's analysis that it breaks ground for an understanding of history more appropriate to the New Testament by removing history "from the range of man's arbitrary choice" and allowing responsibility to be grounded in the call of man's being in the world. Since in the Heideggerian understanding man can only respond to this call with himself, a responsibility is rediscovered "that is like the responsibility which the Christian faith makes available to man when it opens up the historical character of human existence." [46] We need to keep in mind, however, that the context of this endorsement of Heidegger is Gogarten's defense of Bultmann against his conservative Luther critics. Actually, the primary reason for the change in Gogarten's concept of history lies in the relative absence of the eschatological dimension from his Thou-I discussion and his conviction that Christian faith secularizes and historicizes the world by turning it over to the responsibility of man. Gogarten states quite clearly that we are only at the beginning of developing a concept of history more adequate to the theological task.[47] And he adds that if anyone

[45] *Ibid.*, p. 100.

[46] EK, pp. 60-61 (Eng. tr., pp. 60-61). Gogarten believes Heidegger's understanding of history is more appropriate than either that of positivism or idealism (Troeltsch and Dilthey). The latter, he believes, ends up with a version of the divine immanent in the human which makes responsibility a matter of human self-determination rather than of genuine response to another (*ibid.*, pp. 40-41; Eng. tr., pp. 32-33).

[47] EK, pp. 60-61. (This comment is from the Foreword to the second German edition and was not translated.)

does not like Heidegger and can learn to overcome elsewhere the dominance of the subject-object style of thinking, he has no objection. But learn it we must—not because this is the latest philosophical fashion or even because it is the inherent tendency of the post-modern world view—but because Christian faith itself historicizes existence in a way that undercuts subjectivism.[48]

As close as he stands to Bultmann in his general outlook, Gogarten places his emphasis differently. He is less explicit than Bultmann on the hermeneutical problem of how we in fact move from our present self-understanding into the thought world of the New Testament.[49] But Gogarten's real concern lies more in the *critical* analysis of the contemporary self-understanding than in the way we can translate the gospel into the language of our time. Gogarten believes the greatest danger facing the church is that the gospel will be identified with some form of the law of the contemporary world (or, worse yet, with that of some past world). In the face of this threat the preacher and theologian cannot carry out their responsibility simply by preaching and teaching verbal orthodoxy, since their words will inevitably be understood in the context of the contemporary self-understanding. Neither can they simply translate the gospel into the contemporary self-understanding, but they must translate *against* it, in such a way that the gospel will not be preached as a law, whether Christian or modern. Whether the gospel is *heard* or not rests with the Holy Spirit; but the theologian cannot use the Holy Spirit as an excuse to avoid learning to

[48] EK, p. 57 (Eng. tr., p. 52).
[49] In his later work Gogarten talks about the theologian's task as one of keeping the church in living contact with the historical situation by carrying on the constant process of "translation." This translation, he says, can only be carried out if the theologian is "at home" in his world and learns to think in the "foreign language" of the New Testament world (WIC, pp. 7-10). Unfortunately, Gogarten does not tell us *how* one comes to be able to "think" in the "foreign" language.

speak insofar as humanly possible so that it is the *gospel,* not some kind of world view, that is heard. Thus *the* theme of theology for Gogarten is law and gospel, not simply as a doctrine about which one ought to have the correct views, but as the actual, concrete task of both theologian and preacher. For only so long as Christian faith is open to history is it protected against becoming either a myth or a religion of law. The meaning of the law-gospel theme in theology, therefore, is that "Christian faith may remain faith in the Gospel, and then also be open for historical life without which there is no human being in freedom and responsibility." [50]

The shift in Gogarten's understanding of historical reality is thus both an effort to give greater weight to eschatology and responsible sonship and an effort to more adequately describe the reality medium of contemporary existence. For he is convinced that "God seeks man in the reality in which he lives." [51] The Word of God in Jesus Christ will meet a man in the historical reality of his present existence and that means in "the Law in the form which it has taken here." [52] Gogarten's concern with the way the question of God is raised in our historicity is not an effort to create a natural theology which will serve as a foundation upon which to erect a theology of revelation.[53] On the contrary, Gogarten is seeking to uncover the secular form of the law in order that the church will not point its preaching of the gospel of freedom at a law under which no one is living. By trying to alert the church to the *place* where the question of God becomes urgent today—man's historicity, Gogarten wants to help the preacher and teacher to maintain the gospel as

[50] MZGW, p. 34.
[51] *Ibid.,* p. 250.
[52] *Ibid.,* pp. 249-50.
[53] This effort to understand the "natural" man prior to faith but on the basis of the revelation could be called a "natural theology" only in the sense Bultmann gives to the term. Cf. Bultmann, *Glauben und Verstehen I* (Tübingen, 1933), 294-312.

"pure" gospel. If the church lacks an understanding of the secular form of the law, it may end up turning the gospel into a law of some kind even though it can theoretically distinguish law and gospel and takes great pride in talking about justification by faith. Gogarten's purpose in dealing with the hiddenness of God in history, therefore, is not to make unbelievers into believers as a basis for their eventually becoming Christian, but to keep the church from making believers into unbelievers by turning their attention to an idol dressed in the garments of Christian doctrine and Christian ethics.

3

The Hidden God

It remains for us to make explicit the connection Gogarten finds between the question of God and the question of man as it arises in our historicity. From what we have said about Gogarten's understanding of historical reality, it is evident that the question of God will be put to man at the point of his responsibility for the world before the mystery of the oncoming future. This mystery is by nature absolutely unavailable to man, since no matter how great his technological advances, he will never be able to embrace the totality of the future. Indeed our tremendously expanded ability to control great stretches of the proximate future has only made us feel more acutely the threat of the infinite future which interminably bears down upon us. Because it is absolute mystery, Gogarten can say that man, when he lets himself be put in question by this impenetrability, exposes himself to the "oncoming futurity of God" (*Gottes Zukünftigkeit*).[54]

Today it is popular to say that the word "God" is moribund, a worn-out coin whose value is no longer negotiable. More

[54] VH, p. 181. This difficult expression is usually translated "oncoming future of God" although occasionally some other expression such as "God's imminent advent" or "God's inbreaking presence" may be used.

important is *why* this word has become shallow and uncompelling. From the perspective of Gogarten's thought, this name has collapsed not because the proofs of existence have failed or the attributes have been shown to contradict one another, but because our language about God has lost connection with the reality we experience in our own history. "God," however, is the word we have, and Gogarten continues to use it to name the absolute mystery which presses upon man's consciousness of responsibility for the world. The reason why the question of God is genuinely raised only when a man becomes aware of the mystery which puts his humanity in question is that the reality toward which the word "God" points is an

impenetrability and inexpressibility; it means a majesty of unthinkable brilliance; it means a farness and nearness, that is nearer to us than we are to ourselves. And it means all this as that on which we call because without it we are not men. For no one can name God seriously without at the same time confessing himself to depend on him.[55]

Or as Gogarten put it in one of his earlier works, to "encounter God is to encounter Him in everything as the power which has me in its power." [56]

Gogarten's understanding of the Godhead derives from Luther's powerful interpretation of the awful majesty of God as the *inquietus actor* who drives all creatures.[57] To speak of God apart from experiencing his power in our lives and in all that is and comes to be is to miss his reality entirely. For this is not a power with which a man may or may not concern himself as it pleases him, but the power which defines and em-

---

[55] Gogarten, "Entscheidung im Nichts," *Eckart,* 1952, p. 300.
[56] Friedrich Gogarten, *Der Zerfall des Humanismus und die Gottesfrage* (Jena, 1937), p. 30.
[57] In this connection, see Gogarten's essay, "Glaube und Sittlichkeit in Luther's Schrift *De servo arbitrio*," ZThK, 1951; pp. 229-64.

powers his selfhood, his existence as man.[58] Of course the "power" or "mystery" Gogarten intends here is not a special object of experience, nor is it particularly connected with a sense of the sacred. On the contrary, it is the power of the question of man when that question reaches the intensity of demanding an answer which man can only give with himself. Thus God is not a being which uses the oncoming and impenetrable future; he is himself that which comes.[59] But we must remember that the future Gogarten means here is the absolute future which throws man back upon his naked selfhood. If a man does not succumb in resignation or despair, nor flee into the security of an ideology or the amnesia of hectic activity, then he must answer its interrogation with himself. It is precisely here where man is strongest, where his being the creator and preserver of himself and the world is at stake, that he stands under the pressure of the question of God.

Of course, the question put to man by the future will not be experienced explicitly and directly as the "question of God." Why should it ever occur to one who experiences this acute summons that it might be "God" challenging him? How could such a thought occur to him since there is no place more "God-less" in the religious sense than where man is aware of his responsibility for the world—there man is alone.[60] For Gogarten it is precisely the nature of God to be hidden in this way, to deal with man where he least expects it. God is present not only where "the Holy" seems most potent and man appears neediest, but where man is most self-reliant and most

[58] WG, p. 35 (Eng. tr., p. 37). See also Gogarten's *Politische Ethik* (Jena, 1932), pp. 7-8.

[59] VH, p. 177.

[60] To believe in God is not to believe there is "a god," or to hold a particular view of the nature of this being and its attributes. Such concepts have "meaning for the man of today only insofar as he has gotten into the burning question of man. But once he has gotten into it, then all these concepts vanish like the snow before the sun" (Gogarten, "Entscheidung im Nichts," *Eckart*, 1952, pp. 300-301).

profane. The only way this pressure of man's responsibility will be *known* as the work of the hidden God is through the Word of the revealed God, Jesus Christ. And if the church is alert to its task it will aim this Word at the actual law of autonomy and responsibility under which men are living today. Then it will both confirm and intensify the demand of this responsibility to the point that the man who hears this address will become aware of his refusal of the mystery which approaches him.[61] Then for the first time he will know that the power which challenges him is the hidden God. But then he will also know the real meaning of the word "God," namely, "he who makes alive the dead and calls what is not that it may be." (Rom. 4:17; my transl. of Gogarten's rendering.)

But even here in Jesus Christ—Gogarten would say, especially here, God is hidden and unavailable to man.[62] Thus the hiddenness of God has the same dual character as the Word of God which always meets us as law and gospel, gift and demand.[63] On the one hand it is God's hiddenness in his creation as the consuming fire which may break out on man at any moment; on the other it is God's hiddenness in Jesus Christ where this same fire is seen as his burning love for the creature. From the fact that God is most hidden in his revelation, it follows that there can be no direct ("natural") knowledge that it is God who meets us in the history of Jesus. If God does indeed make himself heard by man through Jesus, it is a totally contingent happening, occurring out of the "density" of this history. For the hiddenness of God means that we cannot know God on the basis of anything other than God himself. Therefore, if we are to speak authentically of "what our language intends when it says 'God,'" we must know

[61] MZGW, pp. 252-53.
[62] Gogarten, *Der Zerfall des Humanismus*, p. 16.
[63] Gogarten, "Wort Gottes und Schrift," *Deutsche Theologie*, 1936, pp. 210-211, 215-18.

that the "freedom to speak of or to God can only be received from God Himself who continually makes man free for Himself." [64]

The freedom to address God is the courage to let ourselves be grasped by the uncanny power which surrounds and penetrates our being in the world before the oncoming future. Such a courage, in which man "must open himself in the darkness, in the mystery of God that threatens to destroy him," is what Gogarten means by faith.[65] Wherever, in other words, a man seeks the courage to remain genuinely responsible by abiding with the question put to him from the impenetrable future, he enters the question of faith in God. Gogarten is convinced that this question is the presupposition for our hearing the gospel today. For it is only because men actually experience the power of the hidden God that the revelation of this power in Jesus of Nazareth can address their *existence*. Therefore, only when the church ceases to treat the claim of the crucified and risen Jesus as a religious message and begins to see that it concerns the being of man before the mystery of the future will its preaching become authentic. This is why Gogarten says in *The Preaching of Jesus Christ* that wherever we are pushed out of our self-evident truths and securities and experience the uncanny power of the oncoming future, there Jesus Christ is nearest. For only if there remains before us nothing but this "awful other" will we know him as the New Testament intends him, "for he is this other in human form." [66] Wherever therefore the question of God and man is asked in earnest, the question put to us by the history of Jesus will first become meaningful.

There are several problems posed by Gogarten's understanding of the hiddenness of God in history which need to be

[64] WIC, p. 77.
[65] Gogarten, *Der Zerfall des Humanismus*, p. 37.
[66] VJC, p. 21.

considered before we move on to his Christology. First of all we have obviously left unclarified the relationship he finds between historical reality and historical research directed to the past. This was a deliberate omission because the epistemological problem can best be discussed after we have examined his Christology and his concept of faith where the issue is most acute in relation to the historical Jesus. At this point it will be fruitful, however, to ask about the status of the past in Gogarten's thought. Does he not absorb the past into the present by his exclusive concern with a responsibility directed to the future? Actually his later work still treats the past much as it was dealt with in his Thou-I period—as a direct claim on my existence demanding that I respond with myself. Far from dissolving the past into the present, Gogarten would argue that treating the past as a living claim on the present is the only way to let it have its own integrity since an explanation in terms of causal interconnections objectifies the past in such a way as to deaden its power to elicit our response. Of course this still leaves unresolved the problem of combining such a response to the past with the critical acumen demanded of historical research.[67]

No doubt the most problematic aspect of Gogarten's views on the hiddenness of God in history, however, is his concept of mystery. Although Gogarten makes less explicit use of it than we have, usually speaking simply of "God," there are two difficulties inherent in using the notion of absolute mystery or oncoming futurity to designate God. First we have to ask if the concept is sufficiently clear to be really useful in theological discussion. Since it is an "absolute" mystery before which every human effort to penetrate or control must recoil, how can we even speak of it at all except to utter a cry of awe or despair? Gogarten's solution to this problem of theological language is to point to the mystery and discuss it only from

[67] EK, pp. 60 ff. (Eng. tr., pp. 56 ff.). See below pp. 136-46.

79

the perspective of our experience of it. Since from the conceptual standpoint mystery is strictly a limit, the theologian is reduced to a phenomenological description of man's relation to the boundary of his existence. But although what God is in himself remains hidden from man, what God is for *man* is revealed in his Word, Jesus of Nazareth. The fact that God gives himself to man in the person of Jesus means there can be a theological language about God's intention for man which takes the relation of men to one another as its model. In fact one must say that human relationships are more than simply a model, for, as we have seen, Gogarten believes that the relation of the love to God and the love to the neighbor is so intimate that the relation of man to man is not only an analogy for the relation of man to God but *participates* in that relation. There is of course a profound difference, since the relation of a human son to his human father, for example, does not concern his entire being. A man is not only a son but also a friend, husband, citizen, and a father, in turn. Man's sonship before God, however, concerns his being as such; it embraces the totality of his existence so that his being and nonbeing are at stake in it.[68]

But if what God is in himself remains unknown, we must raise a second question about Gogarten's understanding of the hiddenness of God. On what basis can we actually justify calling the mystery or void beyond the limit of man's comprehension by the name "God"? Gogarten sometimes speaks of the pure oncoming future and sometimes of the pure oncoming future of God. How does the second formula differ from the first? Gogarten would have to derive his answer to this question from his conception of the relation of God's hiddenness to his revelation. So long as the man who exposes himself to the impenetrable future is without faith, this future will appear to

[68] VH, p. 43; also MZGW, p. 14.

him solely as an uncanny power threatening his existence. But if he gets the courage through Jesus to expose himself without reservation to this darkness, he will know it as the power of God who calls him into being despite the threat of nothingness. Therefore Gogarten does not mean by "God" the name of something that *uses* the pure future to awaken man's knowledge of his contingency; God does this "work" simply by his presence as the oncoming future and he "speaks" in the same way, not only by sound waves but by his futurity eliciting man's presence and verbal response to him. This identification of God and pure oncoming futurity does not result in pantheism, for this future is absolute mystery and therefore a most appropriate vehicle for expressing the working of the hidden majesty of God. In other words, God is not identical with the *future* but with the unfathomable *mystery* of the future. The same thing could be said of such phenomena as fidelity, trust, love. The advantage of the concept of the future over these is that it can embrace not only the dimension of mystery in interpersonal relations but also what comes to man from all of history and from nature as well.

The obvious question at this point, however, is whether on the basis of the law-gospel pattern Gogarten is not carrying on a *sub rosa* natural theology enterprise which will serve as the basis or, rather, not serve but dominate as the content and final criterion of what we shall be able to say about the revelation of God in Jesus Christ. Of course we ask nothing new; this was the great issue on which the dialectical theology movement foundered in the late twenties and early thirties with the acrimonious debates which pitted Barth against Gogarten and Brunner. Gogarten does not intend to make his analysis of the historicity of man a presupposition upon which everything else is based, but neither does he intend or even think it possible to make Christology a presupposition on which everything is based. No doubt he was thinking of Barth when he wrote that to reverse the order of law and gospel only inverts a misunderstanding of the real import of the problem.[69] Gogarten asserts that neither law nor gospel precedes the other—although, in terms of our explicit knowledge that the power under which we stand in our historicity is God, we do move from gospel to law. Gogarten is aware that in dealing with the world theology runs the risk of being tainted, but he believes the risk must be taken if we are both to preserve the gospel from being turned into a law and do justice to the doctrine of Creation. For both creation and incarnation mean that

the world is not some kind of barrier between God and man from which man must free himself to come into a right relation to God. The world originally belongs to the God relation, indeed in its very center, which is to say in the freedom for God.[70]

Thus Gogarten does not have a natural theology in the sense of a general anthropology upon which all else is based. Rather because man always stands between God and the world, between the gift of the gospel in Jesus Christ and the demands of the world's law, the theologian's situation is doubly dialogical.[71] For the theologian stands under both the single demand of the law which meets him along with the gospel as the one Word of God, and the many forms of the law as it meets him in the world. Therefore he cannot first gain an understanding of the concrete historical form of the law and then interpret the gospel on that basis, nor can he know the gospel in isolation from the historical structures of the world and then "apply" it to the contemporary situation. Neither the laws of the world nor the Word of God as law and gospel are at the disposal of the theologian as though he stood outside their collision. Rather, the "pressing concrete knowledge of the historical hour and the

[69] KW, p. 165.
[70] WG, p. 56 (Eng. tr., p. 58).
[71] MZGW, p. 9.

knowledge of the Word of God happen at once and not one before the other." [72] Given Gogarten's definition of the structure of theological understanding, we can never decide in the abstract whether a theologian has listened to himself and his world more seriously than to the Word of God witnessed in Scripture, but can only judge his actual exegesis and analysis by entering into the theological dialectic ourselves.[73] With that observation we will have to leave off discussing the problem of natural theology and turn toward an analysis of Gogarten's writings on Christology.

[72] KW, p. 183.

[73] EK, p. 10. Even by this standard, however, Gogarten does give his critics some grounds for the "natural theology" charge, since he only gets around to writing about Christology after an extensive anthropological development. In *The Reality of Faith,* for example, he devotes the first half of the book to showing that faith concerns, first of all, the being of man, and only secondarily his action. As he begins his discussion of Jesus' preaching, he explains his procedure with the comment that only because being is the "horizon" in which the history of Jesus occurred has he been able to speak of it in general terms (WG, p. 113; Eng. tr., p. 112).

What have you to do with us, Jesus of Nazareth?
MARK 1:24

III

THE HUMANITY OF
JESUS CHRIST

1

The Historical Reality of Jesus

The name "Jesus" is an embarrassment. Although we can talk of Moses or Muhammad with a sense of reality, the conversation becomes uncomfortably slippery when the name Jesus turns up. This uncertainty persists depite the century and a half expended on ferreting out the "real" Jesus in his full humanity. Gogarten believes the effort failed because the power of Jesus' humanity in the church has always been drawn from faith in his divinity. Ironically the net effect of the old liberal effort has also been to dilute the force of his manhood, since as one of the great men of history who have shaped its course by their creative will, Jesus offers little that could not be found elsewhere. If we are not misled by the absentminded recitation of formulas in the churches, it is no exaggeration to say that for increasing numbers of men the name Jesus is an empty form.[1] Since our subject-centered orientation must look at him as a pattern to be achieved by the realizing-producing subject, the vast majority of the Protestant laity have in effect replaced the sacramental-metaphysical categories of the ancient dogma with the religious-moral categories of modern individualism.[2]

But surely any Christian theology worthy of the name must confess that Jesus is the revelation of God. Gogarten believes this is the claim we actually encounter if we approach the humanity of Jesus as it is presented in the New Testament. For Gogarten the divinity of Jesus Christ is precisely his historicity. In more general terms, "revelation in the sense of the Old and New Testaments . . . happens just where nothing but history happens." [3] It has become a commonplace of contemporary theology that revelation is not the imparting of information about God, but in some sense God's imparting of himself. Gogarten also finds the particularity of the biblical revelation in the *relation* of God to man, and he defines revelation as God's "being with man." [4] This being with man is so intense and intimate that it renders impossible any speculation on God's being in himself. This is why Gogarten insists that the God of the Scriptures is absolutely ungraspable, the final and absolute mystery before which man is questioned and summoned in his very being. It is the same God who is hidden in our historicity and revealed in the historicity of Jesus; although if we are to speak of Jesus as the revelation of God, something different must happen in his historicity than in ours. In fact

[1] VJC, pp. 25-26.
[2] WG, pp. 114-15 (Eng. tr., pp. 113-14).
[3] ZThK, 1953, p. 342.
[4] *Ibid.*, p. 345.

everything depends on Jesus' history being *qualitatively* different since it is finally a matter of the difference between God and man. Yet it is just as essential that this difference be seen *within history* and not cheaply purchased with an appeal to the supernatural. It is in the *humanity* of Jesus that God reveals himself and this humanity is the "sole starting point for our thought about him." [5]

This last phrase indicates Gogarten's characteristic emphasis in contrast to Bultmann's position with which he otherwise shares so much. Gogarten holds that not only what God does in conjunction with the person of Jesus but also Jesus' response to God's action toward and through him is proclaimed by the New Testament as revelation. Although the Cross and Resurrection are central, they must be understood in relation to this *particular* man, so that his preaching and healing become a clue to the meaning of the Cross as well as the other way around. Gogarten is not interested in the personality or character of Jesus, but in his "person." As we have seen, person does not mean inner life or individuality but the being of man in his relation to other men and to the divine mystery. Thus theology is not interested in the psychological make-up of Jesus, because faith itself has no "interest" (in the deepest sense of the word) in his personality but only in his being.

Bultmann also distinguishes between person and personality, but for him the person of Jesus simply means the fact "that" a man named Jesus is confessed as the Christ.[6] Faith has no stake in the "what" of Jesus, since the Cross, proclaimed as the eschatological event, is the content of the Christian message.[7] Bultmann would seem to gain his strongest New Testa-

[5] VJC, p. 31.

[6] Rudolf Bultmann, *Glauben und Verstehen* I (Tübingen, 1933), 259.

[7] Bultmann is willing to admit that Jesus' preaching implies a Christology insofar as Jesus regarded his preaching as a sign of the coming Kingdom (*Ibid.*, p. 204). But even here it is only the fact of his preaching, not the content, which is decisive (*Ibid.*, p. 205).

ment support from Paul who has manifestly little to say about the course of Jesus' life and teaching. According to Bultmann, Paul is interested only in the fact that Jesus was a "definite, concrete man." [8] It was on the question of Paul's concern with the person of Jesus that Gogarten first questioned Bultmann. If Bultmann is right, he objected, then *any* definite, concrete man would have done as well as Jesus.[9] The danger of Bultmann's perspective according to Gogarten is that what happens in the Cross will be mythologized by our ignoring the obedience of the Crucified. Jesus' humanity would then become a neutral material used by God. Certainly Paul is not curious about the historical individuality of Jesus, but he is speaking of Jesus as the person who "has his existence out of God." If Jesus is the "deed" of God in the Cross and Resurrection, then he is God's deed as the Son who *responds* to the Father's call.[10] And we learn of this obedience not only through Paul and the other witnesses but from Jesus' own preaching, for "whatever it says taken in pieces, as a whole it intends his own person." [11]

In a recent discussion of Bultmann's criticism of the "new quest of the historical Jesus," Gogarten agrees with Bultmann that the core issue of the current debate is not merely whether we can establish a continuity between Jesus and the kerygma of the early community, but whether we can demonstrate the

[8] Rudolf Bultmann, *Theology of the New Testament* (New York, 1950), I, 294. In *Jesus and the Word,* Bultmann says that even the name "Jesus" cannot be guaranteed, and therefore he will concern himself only with the "complex of ideas in the oldest layer of the synoptic tradition" (New York, 1958; p. 14). But there is no way of being sure that the historical phenomenon for which Bultmann says he will let the name Jesus stand was *any* "definite, concrete man." And the difference between the "overwhelming probability" that Jesus really was the bearer of the message, and the lesser probability that Jesus pointed to his own person as the incarnation of his message, is only a difference of degree.

[9] VJC, p. 178.
[10] *Ibid.,* p. 179.
[11] MZGW, p. 244.

"inner necessity" of the proclaimer's having become the proclaimed.[12] Bultmann thinks the question can only be answered by the assertion that the early community understood the history of Jesus as the "eschatological event" which brings the possibility of a new existence.[13] Gogarten says this answer evades the issue since Bultmann does not show what basis or justification the community had for transforming Jesus the promiser of salvation into Jesus the savior. On the contrary, Gogarten writes, only if the historical Jesus actually *is* the savior can the community find Christ in his words and deeds. That means the paradox of "life in death" which is the reality of salvation must have been explicit in the preaching and actions of the historical Jesus or, to use Gogarten's preferred term, in the historical (*geschichtlich*) reality proper to him.[14]

Gogarten's initial formulation of his position on the question of the historical Jesus as raised by Bultmann dates from 1948 and obviously foreshadowed the "new quest" at some points. In his most recent discussion of the problem of Christology Gogarten explicitly sides with the new quest, especially the form it takes in Gerhard Ebeling's work. He even accepts Ebeling's definition of the task of Christology: "to bring to expression

[12] JCWW, p. 29.

[13] Rudolf Bultmann, *Das Verhältnis der urchristlichen Christusbotschaft zum historischen Jesus* (Heidelberg, 1961), p. 25.

[14] JCWW, p. 29. For Gogarten, of course, the phrase "the historical (*geschichtlich*) Jesus" does not mean the same thing as "the Jesus of historical (*historisch*) research." Since English has only one word for history, the phrase "historical Jesus" enjoys a built-in ambiguity, referring to both the concrete actuality of Jesus of Nazareth and the biographical constructions produced by research. The ambiguity has been compounded, as James M. Robinson points out, because the nineteenth-century quest of the historical Jesus tended to conflate the two meanings. Cf. *A New Quest of the Historical Jesus* (London, 1959), p. 28. Where the context does not make it clear which sense of "historical Jesus" is intended, I have usually employed a circumlocution such as "the historical reality of Jesus" rather than use a neologism.

what has come to expression in Jesus himself." [15] Gogarten explains that for him this formula, "come to expression," means that something is articulated which has the power "to bear the whole existence of man." [16] In the case of Jesus it is his own faith which came to expression as absolutely decisive for his existence. The task of Christology is to articulate the faith which came to expression in Jesus in such a way that it becomes manifest as the bearer and determiner of our own existence. Gogarten believes this was what the kerygma of the early community actually did; the significance of Jesus was not his "divine nature" but the faith through which he determined the existence of those who believed in him. Since genuine faith, as opposed to mere belief, is something which embraces the totality of a man's existence, the articulation of this faith means at the same time the articulation of Jesus' existence as a whole. Of course that does not mean the totality of particulars, but "his existence in the peculiar wholeness into which it is concentrated and comprehended by the faith which bears it." [17] Although Gogarten grants that the connection between the language of the kerygma and the historical reality of Jesus is lost for us because the modern effort to approach Jesus has a quite different understanding of human existence, he sees no reason to doubt that the early Christians believed the Christ it proclaimed was identical with the historical Jesus. Moreover, even though this kerygma is the only medium of access to the historical reality of Jesus, the kerygma itself expresses "the way faith grasps his existence as a whole." [18]

The modern contrast between the "historical Jesus" and the Christ of faith has its roots in the fact that the kerygma has been thought to refer to the supernaturally endowed being of dogma, and the task of research is to rescue the "real" Jesus

[15] *Ibid.*, p. 33.
[16] *Ibid.*
[17] *Ibid.*, pp. 34-5.
[18] *Ibid.*, p. 37.

from his imprisonment in the creeds. The importance of Bultmann's work for this issue, according to Gogarten, is that he denied both alternatives: he showed that the earliest community was not interested in either the divine nature of later dogma or the religious personality of historical research, but in the "that" of Jesus' having come in the last hour. The usual attack on Bultmann's solution asserts that he has in effect severed the connection between the historical Jesus and the preached Jesus by denying the relevance of the concrete history of Jesus for Christology. But this charge can only hold true, Gogarten believes, if concrete history means nothing but the representation of a man's personality and career. If there were another way of articulating the concrete historical reality of man, it might be possible to speak of the "what" of Jesus without falling into the trap of the "life of Jesus" tradition.[19]

The specific concreteness Gogarten is seeking with regard to the history of Jesus concerns Jesus' *relation* to God and to the world as a whole.[20] Because this relation actually takes place in Jesus' responsibility or faith, it is at once too ordinary and too subtle for the usual categories of historical research. Nevertheless Gogarten believes it must be called historical rather than cosmological or supernatural. To object that it is not historical because the being of God is involved is to miss the fact that the kingdom of God which Jesus proclaims has its place in the midst of the world.[21] Although our access to this history is through the kerygma in which it came to expression for the early community, historical research can help us understand the connection of this kergyma with the historical reality of Jesus since research can isolate the actual sayings of Jesus and a few happenings of his public career and offer a general understanding of the world in which he lived. Of course Go-

[19] *Ibid.*, p. 38.
[20] *Ibid.*, p. 45.
[21] *Ibid.*, p. 121.

garten does not use this research to reconstruct imaginatively a portrait of the personality of Jesus and speculate on how Jesus felt about this or that situation, but he employs it in an effort to understand the preaching of Jesus as a clue to the form of his existence as a whole.

2

The Preaching of Jesus

The core of Jesus' message according to Gogarten is "being out of God." In the chapter on secularization we found it necessary to give a preliminary sketch of the double dimensionality of this being by describing the active and receptive aspects of responsibility as they constitute the personhood of the Christian man. At that point we were primarily concerned with the way Gogarten sees this responsibility secularizing and historicizing human life, especially through Paul's concept of mature sonship. In Jesus' own preaching, however, Gogarten finds the emphasis not so much on the freedom from the elemental spirits, as on the freedom of man for God and the neighbor.[22] This emphasis in Jesus' preaching is not wholly new to the New Testament, in fact Gogarten believes it to be the central theme of *both* Testaments. The particularity of the history recounted in the Old Testament is that Israel lets this history happen in "unconditionally exposing itself to the future which is entirely the oncoming future of Yahweh." [23] Naturally the obedience of Israel includes planning for the future, but here is just where her difference from the Gentiles becomes apparent. The history of the Old Testament people is a continual struggle that their future as a people will not take the place of their future under God, that their being as a people will be "out of God."

According to Gogarten this same struggle lies at the heart of Jesus' own history with the difference that it is no longer the

[22] For Gogarten's view of Paul's relation to Jesus, see VJC, pp. 173-92.
[23] MZGW, p. 396.

91

people who are bearers of the covenant but man as such. In
Jesus' preaching of the Kingdom, the Old Testament contradiction between a self-assured future and the impenetrable future
of God is taken up and sharpened. The Kingdom arrives without any human labor; no one knows the hour—we are to watch
and be ready—and yet the Kingdom is already there although it
cannot be seen. For this Kingdom means the end of an old
reign and the beginning of a new; the end of the life man has
out of his attempt to assure his future and the beginning of a
life lived out of the mystery of the oncoming and incalculable
future.[24] Jesus' announcement of the Kingdom puts men into a
situation of decision—whether to receive their life from the
future of God, or fashion a bulwark against its threatening
mystery with the help of human culture and politics. Put in its
simplest terms Gogarten understands the heart of Jesus' preaching to be the alternative: "Trust in God or trust in the world."
In the one trust, the world stands between God and man and
is used to hold the mystery at bay; in the other, man stands
between the divine mystery and the world open to the mystery
and no longer clutching his worldly form as a buffer against
fate. As Gogarten interprets this basic alternative of Jesus'
preaching, man belongs to God primordially "as only a
person can belong to another . . . in a trust and love which has
its ground in the one trusted or loved."[25] Consequently, to
fulfill the law is not to "do" something as though we had our
being in ourselves and now were to add to ourselves a relation
to God. Rather, the law is fulfilled only when we give God "what
belongs to him—even this, that we are receivers before him."[26]

Gogarten emphasizes that for Jesus the giving and receiving which fulfill the demand of the law do not concern God
and the individual soul, but God and man in relation to the

[24] *Ibid.*, p. 399.
[25] *Ibid.*, pp. 56-57.
[26] VJC, p. 81.

neighbor and to the structures of the world. "The deep meaning of Jesus' command of love is that the revelation of the reality of God has its place nowhere else than in the relation of men to each other, that faith and unbelief are solely determined by the relation to the neighbor." [27] Only when we have seen this, Gogarten adds, will we realize that for Jesus faith is in no sense a theoretical act but the "extraordinarily practical experience of a reality in which God encounters man as his God." [28] The reality Gogarten has in mind is the darkness and void of the deity of God which a man experiences when he allows himself to be torn from his accustomed place in the world and enters a mode of existence which has no visible support, for example, when he loves an enemy. This "darkness or nothingness into which one acts in the love commanded by Jesus," is the "same darkness and nothingness into which faith enters, it is the divinity of God out of which all live, the good as well as the evil." [29]

This indissoluble unity of man's relation to God and to the neighbor is the foundation for Gogarten's case that Jesus made his own person decisive for the kingdom of God, i.e., for "being out of God." Gogarten argues that since Jesus points to the relation of men to one another as the place where God deals with them, this means that his own relation to others is a medium for God's work. Gogarten draws two consequences from this: 1) Jesus binds himself to his fellowmen in the same openness in which he receives himself from the mystery of the impenetrable future of God, and 2) this mystery itself is present for man in Jesus' openness to it. Gogarten concludes that Jesus showed in all his activity a consciousness of being sent by God in the last hour, not simply to talk *about* a life of openness to

[27] *Ibid.,* p. 115.
[28] *Ibid.,* p. 107.
[29] *Ibid.,* pp. 111-12.

the oncoming future of God, but to let such a life occur through his preaching and healing.[30]

In his most recent work on Christology Gogarten develops this same argument more fully. His basic intention is to demonstrate the inner necessity of Jesus being proclaimed as the Christ by showing that he actually showed in his own life the openness before God and the responsibility for the world which was the content of his message. Gogarten supports his case entirely through an analysis of Jesus' preaching. The principle here is that "most statements of Jesus are understood in their full sense when we consider that they intend not only those to whom he says them, but that they hold good no less for himself." [31] Although in this book Gogarten presents the content of Jesus' preaching largely as we have described it above on the basis of his other writings, he does add one important interpretive concept: man's "personal world" (*je eigene Welt*). In contrast to the world as it is viewed in modern historical writing, for example, the personal world of man does not concern the general forces and movements but the specific destiny of the self.[32] Whenever something befalls a man that throws him into a decision concerning his being as man, he experiences his personal world, and the "existing world" (*bestehende Welt*)

[30] Although Gogarten will admit that Luke 4:16 might have been structured by the early community, he feels it in no sense to be contrary to Jesus' preaching as a whole in which Jesus refers to himself as sent in the last hour with the deciding word (*ibid.*, p. 124).

[31] JCWW, p. 194.

[32] *Ibid.*, p. 142. Although the translation "personal" world is not entirely a happy one for "*je eigene*," each of the alternatives such as "proper," "very own," "individual," or the neologism "ownmost" used in translating Heidegger, has its drawback. If I am not mistaken, Gogarten is talking here about the same phenomenon he meant by speaking of the "density" of biblical history. The drawback of "personal" in this respect is that it may convey the idea of "inwardness," whereas Gogarten intends to cover much more than man's private experiences as can be seen by his emphasis on the "neighbor" and the "world." The personal world of man is anything but a world within the individual but rather the world of *concrete relationships* which determine the person.

loses its grip on him. According to Jesus' preaching the place where man experiences his personal world is where he meets a neighbor whose need becomes in that situation the determinant of his destiny—as in the story of the good Samaritan. In the existing world the personal destiny of individuals is considered insignificant unless they come to have an important quantitative influence on technology, politics, or culture. But since the standard of measure for man's personal world concerns his mode of existence before God and the world as a whole, his destiny can be at stake in the most ordinary experiences of life.[33]

With this concept in mind we can go on to consider the three stages in Gogarten's demonstration that Jesus exhibited in his own existence the faith which is the content of his preaching. The first and most important piece of evidence is that Jesus offered no legitimation for his preaching in terms of the existing world of his time, e.g., he made no claim to Messianic authority or power as it was conventionally understood. This in itself indicates that insofar as his preaching was concerned he himself had to choose between the coming Kingdom (trust in God) and the existing world and its law (trust in the world).[34] That he actually chose the former is not only confirmed by his refusal to "prove" his authority but also by his association with the excluded, especially the "sinners." For by proclaiming the kingdom of God as now breaking into the world in his own unauthorized preaching and at the same time linking himself with sinners, Jesus breaks with the law of the existing world— specifically the cultic legal piety of his time. By these two decisions Jesus "shuts himself out of this world and is now himself one of the excluded. . . . What supports him therefore and what he can alone rely on is the coming kingdom of God." [35]

[33] *Ibid.*, pp. 142-43.
[34] *Ibid.*, p. 94.
[35] *Ibid.*, p. 104.

The second step in Gogarten's demonstration concerns Jesus' personal world. Since the concept of personal world refers to the place where a man's destiny before God concretely meets him, the destiny of Jesus as seen in his preaching must concern his mission as proclaimer of the Kingdom. But this destiny meets him as one who must proclaim this Kingdom to those who are living under the power of the existing world, either as those who are successful in it or as those who have failed and are excluded. In this situation the need through which Jesus is called to become a neighbor is not like that which meets the Samaritan, the need of an individual man, but the need of a people to be freed from the power of the cultic-legal piety which deafens both the successful and the excluded to the promise of the Kingdom.[36] Gogarten explains Jesus' understanding of this need through the concept of the fateful entanglement (*Verhängnis*) which binds man and the world. In our discussion of the origin of secularization, we mentioned the phenomenon Gogarten intends by this term when we pointed out that "sin" means man's turning from the worship of God to the service of cosmic powers, which results in man's becoming responsible *before* the world rather than *for* it. Given the primordial character of this inversion, there is no way for man and his world to escape it since men believe that by fulfilling the demands of the law of their world they are pursuing the course of truth and justice. Most serious of all, man cannot even know he has exchanged the truth for a lie since his reversal of the fundamental relation in existence concerns his *being* so that everything he does or thinks is determined by his inverted orientation.[37] By responding to this need of man and taking it on himself Jesus becomes in effect the "neighbor" of man and the world.[38]

---

[36] *Ibid.*, pp. 158-59.
[37] *Ibid.*, pp. 66-67. On *"Verhängnis,"* see n. 44, p. 98.
[38] *Ibid.*, p. 161.

The question which immediately arises at this point, however, is whether such an enormous understanding of one's personal world and destiny is not the height of blasphemy for any man. Gogarten answers this by pointing to the *way* in which Jesus takes on himself the responsibility for the fateful entanglement of the world. Jesus does not claim any special power in himself or a special relationship with God, but bears this responsibility in the same obedience of faith which his preaching demands of all. That Jesus actually was responsible in this way is seen in the fact that he does not regard the fateful entanglement as something which hangs over others alone but puts himself under it in solidarity with his fellowmen.[39] Gogarten illustrates Jesus' unity with the world by contrasting his way of preaching with that of John the Baptist. John speaks of the Kingdom as a coming judgment and relates to men as a preacher of judgment and repentance; Jesus speaks not only of judgment but of a turn in the world's destiny which is beginning in his own preaching and relates to men as the preacher of the good news of God's joy over repentant sinners.[40] And the sign for what is happening in Jesus' preaching—and for his solidarity with the world under the fateful entanglement which affects all—is his association with sinners and outcasts. For in this act the existing world is in fact overturned.[41]

The third step in Gogarten's demonstration, that Jesus manifested the responsibility before God and for the world which was at the heart of his own message, concerns Jesus' relation to God. Gogarten takes as his basic clue Jesus' statement, "ask and it shall be given," which he interprets to mean that, whatever the specific occasion of the asking, man is always completely dependent upon God. Gogarten believes Jesus also understood faith in this absolute sense, since the "all things"

[39] *Ibid.*, pp. 167-68.
[40] *Ibid.*, pp. 181-83.
[41] *Ibid.*, p. 187.

which are possible to faith can be done only by God himself. The relation to God which comes to expression here is that man is right in regard to God when he is a receiver.[42] The fact that Jesus did not speak of his own faith is no reason why we cannot apply his message to himself, for there are actually only two ways such an absolute faith can come to expression: 1) either by calling people into it and speaking of its life-giving power, or 2) by turning with one's whole existence to God.[43] To speak of Jesus' faith, therefore, we must look for the occasion where his destiny is most acutely in decision. One reason so few happenings of Jesus' life are reported is that a single occurrence dominates his life—the fateful entanglement which reigns over man and the world and its collision with the coming Kingdom. The way in which Jesus experienced the action of God in himself, therefore, is "in the asking and believing which were awakened by this happening (*Schickung*) and this destiny (*Geschick*)."[44] Thus Gogarten concludes that the salvation of the world is Jesus' own salvation, since the world's destiny is turned by his relation to God and God's relation to him. For what God did to the world in Jesus had its basis in Jesus' faith.[45]

Gogarten resolves the problem of the "inner necessity" of

[42] *Ibid.*, p. 193.
[43] *Ibid.*, p. 197.
[44]*Ibid.*, p. 207. Throughout his work Gogarten employs the nuances of several German words whose meanings overlap and for which it would be possible in different contexts to use the same English word. *Geschick, Schicksal, Verhängnis,* and *Schickung* can all be translated "fate." In order to keep them sorted out according to Gogarten's usage, I have tried where possible to translate *Verhängnis* by "fateful entanglement," *Geschick* by "destiny," *Schicksal* by "fate," and "*Schickung* by "happening." In the above passage *Geschick* means the experience in which man's existence as a whole stands in question, a question which he can only answer by either refusing this destiny or by submitting to it. *Schickung* refers to manifold occurrences both good and evil in which he becomes aware that his life is not fully in his own hands. Thus it is in the *Schickungen* (happenings) of life that one's *Geschick* (destiny) announces itself. *Ibid.*, p. 148.
[45] *Ibid.*, p. 210.

Jesus the proclaimer becoming Jesus the proclaimed by understanding Jesus as the "pioneer and perfecter" of faith through whom faith becomes possible for all men. The most striking methodological feature of his argument is that it is based exclusively on an internal interpretation of Jesus' preaching. But what is most striking about the content of his argument is that faith can arise not only from the kerygmatic message of the Cross but also through Jesus' preaching. This motif has been most incisively expressed in a compressed passage of *The Reality of Faith* where Gogarten decribes the connection between Jesus' preaching and the "being out of God" of those who hear him. The call of the divine, Gogarten says, which Jesus hears in the same way other men hear it, always "calls man to be, . . . and to be *there* (*da*) where God calls." Because Jesus' own preaching arises from the hearing of this call, "Jesus' own hearing and being *there* (*Da-sein*) where God calls, resounds as God's own call." As a result "every man may participate in the being out of God by hearing Jesus' preaching." Thus Jesus' call to discipleship intends infinitely more than the requirement to make Jesus an example for action; rather, it intends "this immediate participation in the being that has become manifest in Jesus and his preaching." [46] More remarkable than the Heideggerian echo here is the fact that "being out of God" is not made to depend on the Cross and Resurrection in this passage but can be received through the *preaching* of Jesus. Gogarten is not denying that the Cross-Resurrection is decisive but is saying in effect that the *same* event, the same presence of the divine mystery as the "light of grace" is met there as is met in Jesus' preaching. For the actual Jesus of past history is not only the preacher of the Word, he *is* the Word of God. The decisiveness of the Cross-Resurrection is not, therefore, to be played off against the preaching of Jesus, rather it is decisive as the *fulfillment* of Jesus' obedi-

[46] WG, p. 118 (Eng. tr., pp. 116-17).

ence (his being out of God in responsibility for the neighbor), and also as the *divine confirmation* of this "work" of remaining in the sonship which God has given him. But in order to see how Gogarten carries out this continuity between Jesus the preacher and Jesus Christ who is preached, we must turn to his interpretation of the apostolic message.

3

The Responsibility of the Son

Within the variety of New Testament Christologies Gogarten discerns a common theme: the "decisive act of God in Jesus Christ bringing wholeness (*Heil*) to the world and to man." [47] Gogarten emphasizes that this recovery of wholeness is not something which happens to individuals through their relation to Jesus but is the restoration of the *world* to its being out of the mystery of God. Accordingly, the early community was not interested in Jesus' personal qualities, such as his "deep sympathy" for the oppressed or his speaking and acting with "astonishing sovereignty." The historical basis of their message is rather the "form of a man provided with the divine power which rules the world," who by this power frees the world from its introversion.[48] Among the apostolic designations of Jesus' power to fulfill this responsibility and turn the destiny of the world, Gogarten finds the title "Son of God" the most suggestive for a historical as opposed to a metaphysical Christology. He is convinced that the New Testament itself does not mean this sonship genetically or substantially but relationally. For biblical clues to the relation character of sonship he turns to the Old Testament references to the King of Israel and to Israel itself as God's son, and to the New Testament references to all believers as sons through Christ. Gogarten finds in the Johannine concept of the "sending" of the Son, however, the

[47] JCWW, p. 39.
[48] *Ibid.,* p. 41.

most appropriate historical expression for Jesus' vocation as the preacher of the Kingdom. For the Gospel of John makes it clear that Jesus is not sent to reveal the Father's will simply through his preaching and healing, but that his being sent is itself the revelation of God's love for the world. Since the incarnation of the Word is not a single delimited act but embraces the totality of Jesus' life, Gogarten can say that the unity of the Son and Father actually takes place in the sending, and that means in the historical being of this man Jesus of Nazareth.[49] For the specific content of the sending, Gogarten turns to another characteristic Johannine phrase: "not of himself." The meaning of Jesus' being "sent" or his being the Son is that all he is and does springs from his being out of God and not from what he is in the world. Therefore, the history which takes place between the Father and Son takes place in the being of Jesus and concerns the question of man as it is put to Jesus by his destiny as the preacher of the Kingdom. Accordingly, when Gogarten turns to the Cross and Resurrection, he does not deal with them as supernatural occurrences outside the realm of other events or as bits of first-century chronology; rather, he sees the central interest of the New Testament to lie in the history which occurs between the Father and the Son and the world in the sending of Jesus.

The key to Gogarten's interpretation of the apostolic message of the Cross and Resurrection is his understanding of the fateful entanglement in which the world is caught due to man's inversion of his responsibility before God into a responsibility before the world. As we have seen, even the attempt to escape this inversion only gets man more deeply enmeshed since the more he tries to establish the wholeness of his being before the oncoming future the more tightly he is bound by the fearful effort to secure his existence against its threat; consequently, he cannot even know that he has "exchanged the truth of God for a lie." And yet, although he inverts his essential being, this refusal of the mystery cannot undo his nature, but clings to him as his "unnatural being" or his "forfeited" sonship. Since this inversion touches not only all that man himself does but even poisons his perception of the divine mystery and the being of the world as inheritance, the "creative promise of God which calls that which is not into being becomes the annihilating voice of the hidden God which conjures up nothingness." [50] Now the mystery is experienced as wrath.

By "wrath"—which Gogarten interprets via Luther's translation as "zeal" (*Eifer*)—he does not mean a passion in God but the intensity of the mystery from which man receives his life as it is experienced when he turns away from it. This same zeal is experienced as love when man lets it come to him and receives his being out of it.[51] The wrath of God is neither a happening in God nor a purely subjective experience in man but the character of the relation between God and man when man has shut himself against the mystery of his being. Because of the essential connection between man's relation to God and his relation to his fellowmen, the wrath is experienced most acutely in the alienation of men from one another. This is eminently true of Jesus who receives his being as person in his openness to God and his fellowmen. Those who set their trust on what they can make of themselves in the existing world cannot support the presence of one who is apparently indifferent to the claims and demands of this world, and they must oppose him with the passion of men whose existence is threatened— not by any one thing he does or says but simply by what he is.[52] It is in the crucifixion, therefore, that the deadly opposition between his being as person and the inverted being of man and the world reaches its climax.

[50] WG, p. 58 (Eng. tr,. p. 60).
[51] VH, pp. 57-58.
[52] VJC, p. 150.

Through the Pauline motif of wrath (and the corresponding "curse" [53]), Gogarten understands the *event* which takes place in the Cross as far more than the crucifixion of a man. Not "more" in the sense that the bodily agony and death could be dispensed with, nor "more" in the sense that a "meaning" needs to be added to the crucifixion, or that a "supernatural" event takes place along with it. Rather, the crucifixion is included in the total event of the Cross which is the judgment of God on man's inversion of his own being and the being of the world. For in the Cross the fateful entanglement which dominates man works out its final implication on Jesus and at the same time on the world which brings Jesus to the Cross. Yet the world literally does not know what it does in destroying Jesus since it is ignorant of the servitude which drives it on. But Jesus, who takes this destiny on himself in responsibility for those who are entrapped by it, sees through its power as the inversion of being and knowingly lets it come over him.[54] In the presence of *this* death—the nothingness or wrath which lies over the world as a result of the inversion—Jesus "remained the receiver which he is before God; he opened himself to him in trust and obedience." [55] Therefore, the kerygma can also confess that in this obedience of Jesus God has shown himself to be "he who makes alive the dead and calls what is not that it may be." In *this* life—in the "being out of God" which Jesus exposes to the death of the Cross—death itself loses its power to kill and gives way to resurrection:

The life that is lived out of God's sovereign goodness in pure receptivity and gives itself, in this obedience to God, into wrath and death, is accepted and confirmed by God as life received out of him. That is what happens in the appearances of the Risen One.

[53] In *Was ist Christentum?* Gogarten offers an extensive "historical" interpretation of the Pauline concept of the "curse." Cf. WIC, pp. 19-27.

[54] JCWW, pp. 57-58.

[55] VJC, p. 159.

This life shows itself to the disciples—whose world-bound faith in him as the Messiah is broken on his crucifixion and who betray and desert him—as life that has the power to send them out of this death and thus to open in them a faith and trust that is conscious of not being bound by any limits or conditions set by the world.[56]

Gogarten is quick to add that this "life" must not be thought of as an idea about a certain kind of life which the disciples picked up from Jesus' preaching and now apply to him, but as the form of Jesus' being as person, his *being* the Son. Because Jesus entered the dread and judgment of this particular death in openness and trust, "he is able to give others the possibility of opening themselves to this world-free humanity which is lived out of pure receptivity." [57] The event which is designated "Resurrection," therefore, is the actual presence of this new life in its power to awaken the same life in others.

On the question of whether this Resurrection included the actual resuscitation of a corpse which was "seen" in some manner by the disciples, or included at least a vision of some kind of glorified body, Gogarten remains neutral. This neutrality is not a concession to the idea that the modern world view makes it impossible to believe in a physical resurrection—after all, strange things are happening all the time and it is theoretically possible that someone could be pronounced biologically dead and yet recover. But that would hardly make such a person the Word of God which "turns" the inversion of the world's being. What *happens* in the Resurrection—as what happens in the life and death—is not something which can be seen and measured, since its essential dimension occurs between Jesus and God and the world. Any external events corresponding to this invisible event between God and Jesus were determined by "the world view and psychic constitution of the disciples

[56] *Ibid.,* pp. 160-61.
[57] *Ibid.,* p. 161.

and therefore are indifferent to the real happening." [58] Nevertheless, the Resurrection is an event which has its own being apart from the disciples' perception of it. And that event is Jesus' "turning" of the inversion of man's being and the being of the world back to their original being out of God through his obedience. Thus the Resurrection is the manifestation of the love of God in the midst of the wrath and death. As an event between God and Jesus and the world, it cannot be *known* as Resurrection apart from faith, since the medium in which it occurs is that of a humanity which is lived in complete receptivity before God. Although the Resurrection is not a "miracle," it *is* the "wonder" of God in the sense that this event in which there is no direct sign of divine intervention is nevertheless the event in which the destiny of man and the world is reversed.[59] When the apostolic writers say that faith is faith in the crucified and risen Lord, Gogarten understands this to refer to two opposing and contradictory ways in which God is known in these events. In the Cross, God is known in the wrath or nothingness which lies over the inversion of being; in the Resurrection, God is known in the love or plenitude of being which raises to divine sonship the man who has descended into the depth of this inversion. What faith recognizes in these two opposed events, therefore, is the *"one* reality of God" who makes alive the dead.[60]

4

Christological Formulation

The central question of Christology has always been "the unity of God and man in Jesus Christ." [61] And this unity must

[58] *Ibid.*, p. 162.
[59] *Ibid.* The concept of "wonder" here is the same as Bultmann develops in *Glauben und Verstehen*, I, 214-29.
[60] WG, p. 128 (Eng. tr., p. 127).
[61] JCWW, p. 1.

be so conceived that both God and man are present in their fullness. The difficulty with the Chalcedonian formula, according to Gogarten, is that it cannot do justice to the full humanity of Jesus since its starting point is the second person of the Trinity, and the humanity is consequently regarded as something to be used for purposes of redemption.[62] Gogarten believes Luther was one of the first to see that both the humanity of Jesus and the divinity of God can be safeguarded only if we begin to think theologically from the humanity of Jesus Christ in which God has revealed himself. Gogarten cites Luther's dictum: "The humanity of Jesus would be of no use if the divinity were not in it. Yet, on the other hand, God may not and will not be found except through and in this humanity." [63] By following up Luther's start Gogarten hopes to articulate in historical rather than metaphysical terms the unity of God and man in Jesus Christ. His Christology, therefore, is concerned with the historical character of the actual mystery of the revelation which the theologians of the early Church did not so much attempt to understand as to "circumscribe while husbanding its character as mystery." [64] For they knew that "here and only here, namely in the hiddenness of the unity of the Father with the Son, does man's wholeness (*Heil*) occur in eternity—and in time," and it was this mystery, which is not only for us (*pro nobis*) but also without us (*sine nobis*) and against us (*contra nobis*), toward which they directed their entire thought and devotion.[65] Because Christian faith has secularized and historicized human existence, Gogarten believes the metaphysical concepts they employed, "despite their venerable and profound qualities," have become empty for us, and we must attempt to describe this mystery in historical terms—not, of course, in order to solve the mystery but to preserve it as

[62] *Ibid.,* p. 235.
[63] *Ibid.,* p. 1.
[64] EK, p. 71 (Eng. tr., p. 71).
[65] *Ibid.*

mystery, albeit as a historical one.[66] Thus Gogarten cannot
be satisfied with asserting a mere conjunction of the act of God
with the historical Jesus but must attempt to circumscribe the
mystery of Jesus' divinity while "husbanding its character as
mystery."

With this background in mind we can turn to one of Gogarten's christological statements which explicitly follows the
Chalcedonian pattern. What the ancient creed expressed in
terms of two natures, Gogarten expresses in terms of two histories. These two histories in their unity constitute the mystery
of the incarnation.

First . . . the event takes place in eternity between God and Jesus
and secondly it takes place in time between Jesus and the world.
We are alluding to the mystery of the first event, the eternal event,
when we speak of it as what takes place between the Father and
the Son. The secret of the second, the temporal event, is what we
mean when we speak of the earthly life and destiny of Jesus. Yet
these two mysteries, these two events, are not of different kinds, but
the single mystery of God's turning to us in Jesus Christ. And
this mystery shows itself to be God's turning to us precisely by
virtue of our never being able or permitted to speak of it except
by reference to the way each history happens in the other. In the
eternal event between the Father and the Son it is the world, we
men, who are intended, and only to that extent does it concern us.
In the temporal history between Jesus and the world, in his earthly
life and destiny, the eternal unity of Father and Son is intended,
and only in this way does the unity of Jesus with the world and
the world with him take place in it. But this unity is in both cases
a historical one.[67]

But how can an event in eternity be called historical? By
"eternity" Gogarten means that the event concerns man's very
possibility of being: the coherence without which his existence

[66] *Ibid.*, p. 72 (Eng. tr., p. 72).
[67] *Ibid.*

falls to pieces. For "only two things can happen between God and man : either life or death, wholeness or disintegration, being or no-longer-being-able-to-be, either remaining or not-being-able-to-remain before the face of God." [68] The designation "in time" on the other hand refers to an event which concerns a man only partially or from time to time and is therefore under his control. The eternal history which takes place between Jesus and God is not a special super-history but that aspect of Jesus' person which is hidden from the probing of an eye oriented to the analysis of externals. It is nevertheless a history, an event that occurs along with the other history which takes place between Jesus and the world. It must be granted, however, that Gogarten's choice of the phrase "eternal event" is a singular one for something he wants also to call historical as opposed to metaphysical, and it has naturally aroused opposition. [69] Since a failure to achieve a historical expression of the central mystery of the faith at this point would seriously damage his whole program, we must examine this understanding of the eternal event more closely.

Gogarten says that we point to this eternal event when we speak of it as an event between the Father and the Son. What is meant here is simply the relation between God and Jesus, a relation whose medium is not that of divine substance but the faith of Jesus. If it occurs in a different dimension than that of Jesus' relation to the world or the temporal event, this dimension is not the supernatural but the personal world of man. The nature of this relation is that Jesus receives his being from God in responsibility for the destiny of the world under the fateful entanglement. Gogarten has also described

---

[68] WIC, p. 23.
[69] Wilhelm Kamlah, "Gilt es wirklich 'die Entscheidung zwischen geschichtlichem und metaphysischem Denken?'" *Evangelische Theologie* (1954), pp. 171-72; Hermann Diem, *Dogmatics* (London, 1959), pp. 271 ff.

this relation in terms of Jesus' "knowledge" of God on the basis of God's knowledge of him. This knowing is not a wisdom which man can realize by his striving—and to that extent it is hidden from the wise and revealed only to the little ones—for it is a knowing which involves man's being. A man cannot be a son without receiving himself from the father and at the same time giving himself to him as his son. It is in this sense that he is only a son insofar as he is "known" by his father as son and in turn acknowledges the father as father. In this mutual giving and receiving "occurs the particular living relationship which is at once fatherhood and sonship." [70] Since God's presence as the oncoming future demands that man remain in his "being known," God's knowing of man is in fact the gift of sonship. But for sonship to occur this gift must be received. Jesus is the "first born of many sons" because he is the one who responded with himself—even to the death of the Cross. But Jesus is not the first to fulfill this responsibility because he is able to achieve more than other men since he would then be only a world-historical hero; rather, he is able to be "the human answer to the oncoming future of God," because "God in his oncoming futurity gives himself to him as to no one else." [71]

Elsewhere Gogarten speaks of this eternal event with the help of his personalistic understanding of the Word of God. Jesus is one with God "insofar as in distinction to the prophets and apostles he is himself the Word." [72] Just as the direct address of another man gives me his person, so God's Word is God's being as person which he has "spoken" to men in Jesus of Nazareth. "Immediately in and with the humanity of this man God speaks his word to us, promises himself to us. To say it another way: the person (*Personsein*) of this man Jesus of

[70] MZGW, p. 240.
[71] *Ibid.*, p. 407.
[72] *Ibid.*, p. 228.

Nazareth is in a certain sense God's person." [73] No doubt Jesus is the "address" of God to us in a way we would never imagine the divine to appear. For God "permits the glory of his Godhead to be manifest just at the place where from a human point of view nothing divine can be seen . . . where there is only an ordinary man who is nothing of himself." [74] And because he is nothing of himself we meet "in him and in the destiny to which he exposes himself" the invisible power of God in his being-for-us.[75] Thus the unity of God and Jesus does not mean a simple identity, since God remains what he is for himself. As the Word of God, Jesus is "God for us, surrounded and preserved by the mystery of God's being-for-Himself." [76]

Just as the one side of the christological mystery is the unity of Jesus and God, so the other side is the unity of Jesus and mankind, his responsibility for the world. For Jesus' knowing of God through God's knowing of him includes his knowledge of his fellowmen (the "brothers") who have surrendered their sonship and denied the Father.[77] Gogarten conceives Jesus' work to be his remaining in the sonship he has received from God as he stands on both sides of the strife between the enmity of the fallen sons and the wrath of God. Although he is the Son, he remains in complete solidarity with his fellowmen. Gogarten's "historical" expression for Jesus' work, therefore, is that the life of Jesus "is ruled by the responsibility of the one for the many." [78] What Jesus accomplishes in this responsibility is to turn the fateful entanglement by bringing to expression its basis in the inversion of being. By articulating this inversion Jesus not only turns it for himself but gives all men the possibility of recognizing their lostness and again acknowl-

[73] *Ibid.*, p. 224.
[74] *Ibid.*, p. 230.
[75] ZThK, 1953, p. 338.
[76] MZGW, p. 228.
[77] VH, p. 53.
[78] WIC, p. 28.

edging God as God.[79] "For in the 'power' in which he not only lives his own humanity, but also lives the destiny of human history in such a way that its true character is revealed, the power of God is at work which alone is able to turn this destiny." [80]

The unity of these two histories is the *obedience* of Jesus, his twofold responsibility before God and for the world. It is this obedience or responsibility that is the event of redemption by which man is restored to wholeness as a person before God and his neighbor, and by which the world is again perceived as inheritance. Of course this responsibility is something which, although called into being by God, must nevertheless be carried out by Jesus in his whole life. Therefore, the event of salvation in which faith believes is this responsibility or obedience as it occurs not only in the preaching of Jesus but in his birth, life and suffering, death and resurrection.[81] And because this "obedience is rendered in these events, what happens in them between Jesus of Nazareth and the world happens in eternity between the Father and the Son." [82]

But we must ask how replacing the notion of two "natures" with that of two "histories" or two "relations" affects the understanding of the difference between Jesus and other men. The difference is obviously not in some special power or endowment of Jesus which makes him in some sense more than a man. Rather, whereas we have perverted our responsibility as sons, Jesus has "fulfilled" it; whereas we have forfeited our genuine historicity, his life remains fully historical because he exposes himself to the impenetrable future without reservation. Although Jesus is an "accidental, historical man like us," our history, if we remain exposed to the future, "can never appear other than the unavoidable darkness of destruction," while

[79] JCWW, 175.
[80] ZThK, 1953, p. 387.
[81] EK, pp. 73-74 (Eng. tr., p. 74).
[82] *Ibid.*

his history is "the incomprehensibility with which the grace of God shines in this darkness." [83]

We may summarize the basic structure of Gogarten's Christology by saying that there is only one history of Jesus, although this history has two distinct aspects. In the person of Jesus both the life of God (the mystery out of which man and the world have their being) and the life of man (who stands on his own as the responsible son) are fully present yet distinct. The unity of these two aspects in Jesus' responsibility is *the history* toward which faith is directed.[84] Here we have Gogarten's way of honoring the christological task of expressing the unity of God and man in Jesus Christ in such a way that both God and man are present in their integrity. Of course he has not solved the problem of Christology thereby, since his sole concern is to point to the mystery in historical-personal rather than metaphysical terms. And there is no doubt that his personalistic categories are less palpable than those of the metaphysical tradition, but so is the language of the New Testament. It is to the dense and, to that extent, ambiguous metaphor of Scripture that he appeals, especially to Johannine piety:

Fatherhood and sonship . . . in their unity are the single element, filled with the divine *Majestas,* in which Jesus lives here on earth. And he lives in this element as the one sent by the Father to the world, in order to take his own . . . into it so they like him may have life in it.[85]

Important as a critique of Gogarten's Christology from a confessional and historical point of view would be, the scope of the present study restricts us to an internal criticism which must

[83] ZThK, 1953, pp. 390-91. For an earlier discussion of the difference between Jesus and us, see *Gericht oder Skepsis,* pp. 115-18.

[84] EK, p. 73 (Eng. tr., p. 73).

[85] *Ibid.* For an earlier christological discussion that foreshadows Gogarten's present position at several points, see his essay "Menschheit und Gottheit Jesu Christi," *Zwischen den Zeiten* (1932), pp. 3-21.

raise several points as to the consistency with which Gogarten has carried out his own intentions. The first question which comes to mind is whether he has adequately accounted for a difference between Jesus and other men which is actually a qualitative one and not merely a matter of degree. If it is said that Jesus remains open to his fellowmen and receives his being as Son through the power of God, this still seems a difference of degree and hardly the difference between God and man that Gogarten himself says is essential. Actually it seems to me that one of Gogarten's finest achievements in his Christology is to have maintained the complete humanity of Jesus Christ and yet shown how he is nevertheless the "first born of many sons." What differentiates Jesus from other men is that they could not know of the fateful entanglement under which they lived, so that in respect of sin there is no question here of a more or less. And yet, even though Jesus knows and does what no other man was able to do, he did not achieve it through some superhuman endowment but because he remained open to the destiny God sent him, namely, the knowledge of the world's fateful entanglement. In fact the way in which he is most unlike us is not in respect of "divine power," "moral perfection" or "religious genius," but of lowliness, and that not as a virtue he realized but as the openness of his whole existence to the oncoming future of God. Thus Gogarten has heeded Luther's advice that we are to seek God *in* the humanity of Jesus Christ, for he finds Jesus to be the revelation of God precisely because Jesus is *the* man who is "nothing" in the world.

But by refusing to speak of the divinity of Christ except in terms of the relation between the man Jesus and God, Gogarten leaves himself open to the charge of having repeated the liberal type of Christology in existentialist and personalistic garb. Schleiermacher, for example, saw man's predicament as how to achieve the perfect balance between activity and receptivity and described the life of Jesus as the historical actualization of this ideal.[86] Jesus, for Schleiermacher, lives in the sinless perfection of one in whom the possibility of an undisturbed identity of the relationship between sensuousness and God-consciousness became actual.[87] Instead of being "obscured and powerless as in us, the God-consciousness in him was absolutely clear and determined each moment . . . so that it must be regarded as a continual living presence, and withal a real existence of God in Him . . ." [88] Gogarten would not find a comparison of his work with that of Schleiermacher wholly noxious since the founder of modern theology was himself on the trail of a historical approach to theology. Yet it would be a considerable oversimplification to identify Schleiermacher's notion of a unitary self-consciousness with Gogarten's concept of person. Gogarten is not concerned with the inner life or subjective consciousness of Jesus but with the fact that his preaching and activity point to a mode of existence before God. The discussion of the structure of Jesus' personhood is not a case of psychological imputation but an interpretation of the anthropology exhibited in the preaching and action of Jesus. The most important difference between Gogarten's Christology and the liberal type is that he does not call Jesus the Son because his relationship to God was more perfect than that of other men, but because Jesus brought to expression the fateful entanglement and bore responsibility for it by remaining "nothing of himself," and thus received the destiny God sent him in the obedience of faith. There is no question here of a "more or less" in relation to God, or of a scale of religious and moral perfection by which Jesus can be adjudged to have realized the ideal.

Despite the liberals' reputation for having elevated the

[86] Friedrich Schleiermacher, *The Christian Faith* (Edinburgh, 1928), pp. 8 ff.

[87] *Ibid.*, p. 383. Schleiermacher is at great pains to insist on the "perfect historicity of this perfect ideal" (*ibid.*, p. 381).

[88] *Ibid.*, p. 397.

historical Jesus at the expense of the Christ, Gogarten believes some elements of the liberal tradition actually missed Jesus' genuine humanity and historicity by applying a Christ ideal to him. He points out that Wilhelm Herrmann, who as much as any modern theologian wanted to base faith on the humanity of the historical Jesus, claimed that even the unbeliever can see the overwhelming power of good in him and thereby come to believe in the risen Christ who is the revelation of God. Thus Gogarten believes Herrmann actually applied an ideal (the "good") to the man Jesus and failed to let his concrete history come to expression, since he made the "content" of faith an idea outside of history.[89] Gogarten's effort is actually to go further than Herrmann and treat both the Christ and Jesus historically. He also hopes thereby to allow the divine mystery its full reality by refusing to treat the divinity of Christ as an ideal and rather let it retain its character as mystery through the notion that it "appears" in Jesus indirectly because he is "nothing" in the world.

This indirectness means that the character of the divine mystery is not unambiguously revealed in the history of Jesus. Although the light of grace is seen in the midst of the darkness of the Cross calling us out of nothingness into being, Gogarten's notion of God as the absolute mystery seems to

---

[89] ZThK, 1953, pp. 375-81. In *Bultmann's* criticism of Herrmann, however, it is not Herrmann's use of the category of the ethical to understand history which is most objectionable, but the idea that we could have a *direct* relation to the person of Jesus through the "impression" Jesus makes. By "describing the 'inner life' of Jesus as an available fact of world history," Herrmann forgets two things, according to Bultmann: 1) that Jesus is the eschatological turning point, and 2) that faith can only be based in the word of preaching (*Glauben und Verstehen*, I, 106). Gogarten, Ebeling, and Fuchs are seeking to carry out Herrmann's intention of making the historical Jesus the basis of faith, although with the help of a different view of history and a different concept of "person" as well as with an acknowledgment of the full importance of the two elements Bultmann mentions. Ebeling is convinced, in fact, that Herrmann has been misunderstood and that we could still learn a great deal from him (*Verkündigung und Theologie*, pp. 76, 124).

exclude a personal center which has the freedom to reveal or hide himself. Therefore, we have no assurance that the mystery may not finally intend nothingness and death. Since revelation cannot be information nor point to a supernatural world beyond our own, the revelation of the impenetrable future as grace can only mean our participation in Jesus' mode of being. At the end of life in "this" world we may open ourselves in trust to the impenetrable future of death, but we are indeed trusting into the unknown. This is no doubt the price that must be paid by a historical theology that will let go of all metaphysical securities. It pictures the Christian existence as courage, but as a courage of hope and not of assurance. For it must look upon the preoccupation with "assurance" as no more than a flight from maturity fostered by a pre-Christian notion of the divine as a providential cosmic power.

The absence of a cosmic power vertically integrating the events of world history also defines the limits of Gogarten's understanding of the "work" of Christ. Because Jesus' work is simply to be the person he is, the Receiver before God who is responsible for his fellowmen, the traditional expiatory notion is excluded since a sacrifice is essentially a cosmic act linking the natural and supernatural. Moreover, given the fact that the wrath and love of God are neither objective nor subjective but designate the character of man's relation to the divine mystery, Gogarten appeals solely to the notion of participation through faith. One cannot help asking at this point if an understanding of Christ's work which makes no use of cosmological or metaphysical categories can do justice to the *objectivity* of the work of Christ. One of the strong points of Gogarten's Christology is the way he is able to articulate the work of Christ in historical categories and yet maintain its "once and for all" character. What happens in Jesus' obedience is the turning of the *world's* destiny and

116

not simply an event whose reality is solely there "for me" as an individual.

Something has happened in the history of God and man which has created a new situation. The power of the fateful entanglement has been broken by Jesus who brought its root to light and thereby turned the destiny of the world. Of course this event is invisible since it takes place in the personal world of man, i.e., it is not a matter of the political or cosmological order but of the existence of man as a whole. This kind of event by happening once in the history of Jesus has the power to happen again and again for each man who, through Jesus' history, lets himself be drawn into the knowledge of the fateful entanglement and of the God who makes alive the dead.[90] Yet as we noted in the discussion of secularization, *one* aspect of the sonship which Jesus makes possible, namely, the freedom from cosmic powers and the responsibility for the world, is an actuality for every man whether he is a believer or not. Therefore Christ's work of liberating men from bondage to the elemental spirits has in fact become effective insofar as we are living in a secularized and historicized world. The other aspect of Christ's work—the courage to remain exposed in an attitude of hope before the impenetrable future—only becomes effective for each man through his personal participation in Jesus' history, that is, through the act of faith.

[90] JCWW, pp. 228-31.

IV

THE REALITY OF FAITH

1

Faith and the Historical Reality of Jesus

In *The Reality of Faith* Gogarten cites Gerhard Krüger's observation that because we see everything "in the light of our self-consciousness," the subject has become the "presupposition of all that is seen." [1] Partly as a result of this primacy of the subject we are obsessed with the problem of finding impersonal standards through which to reach the objectively real. Accordingly, theology is tempted to demand that revelation be linked to solid historical facts lest it be considered the arbitrary decision of the subject. But as Gogarten showed in his defense of

[1] WG, p. 33 (Eng. tr., p. 35).

Bultmann, this effort is trapped in the very subject-ist outlook it tries to overcome since the separation of the event into an objective fact and a revealed meaning results in a situation where the two can only be held together by an assertion on the part of the observing or believing subject.[2] We have already traced Gogarten's argument that the view of historical reality necessitated by the subject-object scheme is deficient in relation to the concreteness of lived history since the mystery of the oncoming future cannot be made an object for a self-grounded subject but puts the subject in question precisely in relation to its "ground." And yet he is equally insistent that the faith whose absence was partially responsible for the modern drive to aseity, nevertheless fosters a responsibility for all man knows and does. Our task in this chapter, then, is to see how Gogarten is able to combine the freedom and primacy of the subject in the act of faith with the dependence of this act on the prior reality of the "object" of faith.

The source of Gogarten's answer lies in his understanding of the nature of the reality in which the Christian believes. As we have seen, it is the reality of the divine mystery as it manifests itself to the believer in the person of Jesus of Nazareth. Gogarten describes it as a kind of reality which can only be

[2] EK, pp. 46 ff. and pp. 113-15 (Eng. tr., pp. 39 ff. and pp. 88-89). In most cases, however, *revelation* has been seen as a kind of super-history, a "history of salvation" taking place within ordinary world history. This is the approach of the Lutheran critics of Bultmann whose attack prompted Gogarten's *Demythologizing and History*. Eduard Ellwein speaks of the events of revelation as "quite simply superhistorical but . . . occurrences which break into history." Ernst Kinder says the facts of this salvation history are "real in the sense of objective occurrence" yet they are "realities which cannot be established by historical means" (Ernst Kinder, ed., *Ein Wort Lutherischer Theologie zur Entmythologisierung* [Munich, 1952], pp. 26 and 46. These two essays appear in *Kerygma and History*, ed. Carl E. Braaten and Roy A. Harrisville [New York, 1962]). As Gogarten points out, history is treated here merely as a substratum in which revelation "appears," but this is impossible once history has been secularized since it is a single reality. (EK, pp. 46-52 [Eng. tr., pp. 39-46]; see also JCWW, pp. 12-16.)

thought in its unity with the faith it calls into being. Since the nature of faith, in Gogarten's view, depends on this reality our discussion of it must begin with what would ordinarily be called the object of faith. But the peculiarity of this object is that it includes the subject in its occurring from the beginning and for that reason can never be an "object for a subject" but always an "object intending a subject" and therefore not an object at all in the usual sense.

For Gogarten there are actually two aspects to the history in which the Christian believes: the divine mystery before which man already stands, and the personhood of Jesus in whom this mystery shows itself as the power which "makes alive the dead." Our first step in discussing Gogarten's understanding of the object of faith is to see the way in which faith in Jesus involves the prior reality of man's knowledge of the hidden God. Since we are already familiar with the place of the hiddenness of God in Gogarten's thought, we only need to bring it into the focus of the problem of faith. Genuine faith occurs when God has prepared man for it by putting his being in question through the mystery of the future.[3] So long as a man is hard up against the questionableness of his destiny he will be ripe for the decision of faith—not because his existence has become unbearable but because the *question* of his existence has become unavoidable. Consequently Gogarten asserts that faith always concerns the very deity of God, the incomprehensible and unendurable power of the *deus ipse*. The object of faith, the reality in which the Christian believes, is the hidden God who is understood as the power of life through the revelation of God, Jesus of Nazareth.[4]

As we turn from Gogarten's consideration of the prevenient presence of the divine mystery to his understanding of the history of Jesus as the object of faith, we must remember that

[3] ZThK, 1950, pp. 261 ff.
[4] *Ibid.,* pp. 243 and 255 ff.

the medium of this history is the Word of personal relation. Because Jesus lives by the power of God in a decisive sense, his own person is the Word of God to man. As we have seen, the son's being sent, his twofold responsibility to the call of God and for his fellowmen, is the event to which faith is directed. The Word of the event is not a kind of title we can add to a picture in the way we speak of adding a meaning to the facts, but the Word is simply the presence of the divine mystery hidden in the event and inseparable from it. It is an immediate Word of the kind mentioned earlier, a Word in which the One who speaks gives or promises himself, so that to hear this Word cannot mean to believe it is true in the ordinary sense, but to be open to its promise and thereby to "let the word happen." [5] This primordial unity of what can only subsequently appear as fact and meaning is what Gogarten is driving at in speaking of the "word-boundness" of the event or, as he also puts it, the "person-boundness" since it happens "immediately through and to persons." [6] When this intentional inclusion of man is not seen, the actual event which the man of faith perceives is missed and another has taken its place.

If we put the two aspects of the object of faith together— man's experience of impotence before the mystery of existence and the historical reality of Jesus' personhood, we will see that

---

[5] WG, p. 136 (Eng. tr., p. 134).

[6] *Ibid.*, p. 140 (Eng. tr., p. 138). For Luther the "word" is a sacrament through which God works in us what the events signify. A faith which is appropriate to such a word must "let what happens immediately in the word occur in and with its perception of it." WG, pp. 134-35 (Eng. tr., pp. 133-34). Gerhard Ebeling and Ernst Fuchs have developed a concept similar to Gogarten's using the terms "speech event" (*Sprachgeschehen*) and "word event" (*Wortgeschehen*). Revelation understood as a speech event is a matter not so much of the logical as the historical function of the word. It is a word that "meets existence itself in its existing, a word that does not simply offer an answer, but one which awaits, which empowers an answer. This event concerns man himself, that he may be "empowered to exist as answerer" (Gerhard Ebeling, *Wort und Glaube* [Tübingen, 1960], p. 370. Eng. tr., *Word and Faith* [Philadelphia, 1963], p. 352).

for Gogarten the reality which faith perceives involves a knowledge of the divine mystery which is at the same time a twofold knowledge of and with ourselves. Gogarten understands this dual knowledge following Luther who says that before we can understand Christ as God we must understand him as man, for if "one has the man Christ, the man Christ will produce out of his own power the Christ who is God." [7] The knowledge of Jesus' humanity that Luther has in mind here is not a general idea of man—certainly not the biographical-novelistic personality notion typical of modern historical writing—but the concrete reality of our own history in which we strive to secure our world against the corrosion of destiny. To know his humanity together with our own is to see him in terms of the law "written in the heart" of man—the law whose modern form, according to Gogarten, demands that we remain the self-conscious masters of ourselves and the world.

If we hear the "word" of the history of Jesus under the pressure of this law, we will stand under the exigency that all our actions in anticipation of the future be rooted in openness to its impenetrable mystery.[8] Jesus is able to show us our self-imprisonment in the structures of anticipation, because he neither seeks to banish the threat of the future by a new wisdom nor does he throw himself against it in tragic *hubris*. In his freedom and openness to the future's inscrutable darkness and to those who are locked in strife with it, he reveals the fateful entanglement which grips their humanity as modern men. For this entanglement has its root in the inversion of man's responsibility before God into a responsibility before himself. Once the world is desacralized, man can no longer worship the cosmic powers when he turns from God but must find in his own autonomy the final source of responsibility. If the man who stands under the demand of this autonomy comes into contact

[7] ZThK, 1953, p. 383.
[8] MZGW, pp. 250-51.

with the historical reality of Jesus through the witness of the Christian community, his autonomy will be *confirmed* in the sense that Jesus' responsibility is carried out in freedom, i.e., apart from the compulsory power of the law. But the modern experience of autonomy will be *contradicted* by the fact that Jesus is "nothing" in the world since he lives basically from the power of the divine mystery. For a man to know this personhood of Jesus together with the compulsion of the law of autonomy is to become aware that he has refused the mystery. Then Jesus' descent into "nothingness" on the Cross will put such a man in the situation of deciding whether he can remain in this confession of his forfeited manhood, or will once again flee into some form of self-justification, or fall into nihilism. If he decides for the knowledge that he has refused the mystery out of which he has his origin, then he will experience the fact that he "owes" himself to it. This "debt" or "guilt" of himself can only be forgiven when the mystery is present "for" man or, as Gogarten often phrases it, when God "turns" to man. This forgiveness or turning to man happens in the sonship of Jesus, since Jesus' existence as the son, which fulfills itself in his willing entry into the "nothingness" of the Cross, is the revelation that the impenetrable mystery of the future is the "father." [9]

To believe in Jesus Christ through the word of the Cross and Resurrection, therefore, is to "participate in the personhood he reveals." [10] This participation will not be something we perform but will occur through the power of his humanity over our conscience, for a faith that "happens otherwise than through the overpowering of the conscience in the face of sin and death is no faith one can rely on." The reason Jesus has this power is that he turns "the mistrust which motivates the enmity against God back into the knowledge that this mistrust is sin," and at the same time shows our conscience that "we cannot do justice

[9] *Ibid.*, p. 252. See also EK, p. 77 (Eng. tr., p. 77).
[10] KW, p. 110.

to God's zeal by despairing before Him in the knowledge of sin but only by grasping our sonship in the confession of our nothingness." [11] If we believe in this sense, i.e., if we are drawn into the knowledge of the fateful entanglement, we will know that the mystery has "turned toward us" in him. Then we will participate in the Resurrection which Gogarten calls the "revelation and knowledge of God who in the uttermost annihilation . . . has let His life become powerful in the one who comes to nothing before Him." [12] Therefore the divine mystery encounters us *as* this historical man, and to believe in him means to "recognize in the history of this one man our own history and that of all others, and thus receive the possibility of exposing ourselves together with him, unconditionally and apart from every anticipation, to the on-coming future." [13]

Thus Gogarten understands the "of" in the phrase "reality of faith" as both an objective and subjective genitive. The reality is first of all the hidden *divine mystery* which presses man for an answer to the question of his destiny. Of course, this mystery is only fully known as Creator and Redeemer through the Cross and Resurrection, but there can be no genuine belief in God as Creator and Redeemer if it is not connected with this experience of the terrible yet vivifying majesty of the divine mystery. Secondly the reality of faith is *man* as he is driven in his responsibility for the world by the riddle of the oncoming future. And by man Gogarten here means both the man Jesus and all mankind since all stand in the power of God who is "closer to us than we are to ourselves." The reality of faith, therefore, is the conjunction of the human and divine reality in the person of Jesus and through him in the person of every man who participates in Jesus' history through the word of witness.

[11] VH, pp. 61-62.
[12] WG, p. 128 (Eng. tr., p. 127).
[13] ZThK, 1954, p. 354.

2

The Subjectivity of Faith

Our aim is to follow Gogarten's account of how faith can be a free decision of man and yet not have its origin and ground in man's decision but only in the reality which is believed. The first step has been to show that the reality of faith includes in itself the being of the man who believes. It follows that faith cannot be the act of a subject which remains self-contained in the movement of belief. Rather, believing is what we could call an act of being in the sense that Gogarten makes faith a decision prior to all particular acts of decision since it is not a decision *by* the self but *with* the self.[14] This decision is *with* the self because the knowledge of one's directedness to the mystery of the future occurs through the "power of God as the *originating* power out of which man receives his total existence." [15]

Gogarten follows Luther in speaking of this experience of the mystery as a *passive preparation* for faith in the Word of God.[16] Yet even this passive preparation has its active aspect since the readiness of man for faith is not a property automatically bestowed on him but a *relation* to the divine mystery. This can be seen in the fact that man can understand his total dependence in two ways, either as an active preparation he has chosen to recognize with the result that the threatening future remains external, or as what has been effected in him by the mystery with the result that he confesses this impotence as his own.[17] This second understanding arises through the power of Jesus' personhood to draw a man into the consuming fire of the Godhead by virtue of what Luther called the deep, secret yes under and above the no. The relation of the passive and active dimensions of this preparation to faith is that man is called and

[14] WG, p. 35 (Eng. tr., p. 37). Italics mine.
[15] *Ibid.*
[16] ZThK, 1950, p. 261.
[17] *Ibid.*, p. 263.

drawn by the power of the mystery (passive) but that it is up to him to permit himself to be put in question by this call (active). The single act of faith occurs when a man confesses his need and receives his being anew from the divine mystery. In fact Gogarten derives the *certainty* of God's grace from the fact that man's active role in faith means he will be constantly assaulted by the temptation to secure his life against the divine mystery, and the temptation will always keep him conscious of the nothingness of his existence which he must confess before God. This "certitude of my nothingness before God," Gogarten writes, is the "certitude of God's grace," since in the confession of my emptiness I give God what I owe him—myself.[18]

The act of faith proper, therefore, occurs only after man has been "prepared" by the power of the divine mystery which puts him in a situation where an answer is demanded that he can only give with himself. But if he actually responds to this question in the right way his response is not forced by some kind of occult forces working on him, nor is it a special sort of "religious" experience, but it is quite "unambiguously a decision that is demanded of him and that he has to decide in a clear knowledge of why and to what end, an act of judicious obedience." [19] There are three dimensions to this decision, as Gogarten understands it, and in his description of each the uppermost concern is to show how this self-conscious and candid act of the subject is nevertheless grounded in the primordial reality of the object.

The fundamental dimension of the decision of faith is man's *perception* of his forfeited existence before God which we have just described, and at the same time the perception of the new existence opened up to him. Gogarten uses this term "perception" (*Wahrnehmen*) in a special sense. The perception is passive in that it does not create or dominate its object—in fact,

---

[18] *Ibid.*
[19] VH, pp. 67-78.

Gogarten describes it with Goethe's statement, "every new object well observed opens in us a new organ." [20] But the perception is active in the sense that the one who perceives "gives" himself to the reality he perceives, i.e., the object must be well observed in the sense that we do not prevent it from opening in us a new organ. The chief distinguishing mark of the perception Gogarten has in mind is that the reality which is perceived is effectively real in the perception itself. To perceive one's role as a father and act on the basis of this perception, for example, is in fact simply to *be* a father.[21] For Christian faith the new object which creates in us a new organ is the presence of the divine mystery with the world when the world is again known as an inheritance through the sonship of Jesus. Accordingly, Gogarten can define this new organ, faith, as that particular perception in which man, through "the knowledge of the nothingness of his being as he thinks to live it out of his own possibilities, experiences . . . the eternal power and deity of God as His being-for-us." [22] Since the perception is fundamentally the self-awareness which accompanies man's response to the call of the divine mystery in the personhood of Jesus, the being of the one who believes is totally involved in the object of his belief. Once this is understood we can grasp the intent of Gogarten's assertion that the self-consciousness of the man who perceives is in fact the object of his perception, since he "perceives with the being effectuated by God himself in this perception." [23]

The second dimension of the decision of faith simply lifts up a different thematic structure. The perception motif stresses the *self*-consciousness of the decision since faith deals with a reality which "concerns us primordially in our being" and is therefore

[20] WIC, p. 68.
[21] WG, pp. 54-55 (Eng. tr., pp. 56-57).
[22] *Ibid.*, p. 146 (Eng. tr., p. 144).
[23] WG, p. 111 (Eng. tr., p. 110).

always an awareness of the self as called into being by the mystery of existence. Because faith involves man's relation to the mystery in which he already lives even as he lives against it, his faith cannot have the sense of his producing or establishing this relation but only of his *remaining* in the relation into which he has been called and which he now perceives in hearing this call. This second dimension of the decision expresses the active element in faith, the freedom to refuse at any moment the call out of which man now lives. The man of faith does not "believe in" a certain kind of history but his faith is itself

the history in which the responsibility for the world as God's creation . . . permits all events first to be history. That this sonship occurs in the hiddenness of *faith* means that in so far as faith is clearly a decision of man, sonship is not something like a *habitus* or property, but must be continually laid hold of anew in the decision of one's present life. . . . This laying hold of can never have the sense of establishing or appropriating, but is always "remaining" in the sonship newly opened up through Jesus Christ.[24]

The motif of remaining calls attention to the fact that although faith is a self-conscious decision of the subject, the decision does not create the reality which man comes to perceive in his decision, but is a deciding in being decided. The obedience of faith is an obedience of pure receiving and remaining which is so transparent to the call of God that "the decision of man occurring in this obedience is God's creative decision concerning him." [25]

The third dimension of Gogarten's understanding of the decision of faith emerges when we recall that the relation between man and the mystery of existence always includes the world. The *place* of the decision of faith is man's responsibility, since the sonship man inherits through the Cross and Resurrection is ex-

[24] WIC, p. 83.
[25] VH, p. 69.

pressed in a double-edged responsibility *before* God and *for* the world. And yet Gogarten insists that these two modes of responsibility form a *single* responsibility since each mode can only be understood in relation to the other. The receptive or God-ward side of this sonship is cared for by faith; the active or worldly side of sonship is cared for by works. Neither of these aspects in isolation can be the responsibility of an obedient son. A son who refuses to acknowledge his father is no son, nor is one who is not able to stand on his own feet but remains dependent on his father for things he is capable of doing on his own. Yet neither is there the responsibility of a son if the two aspects are confused so that one thinks his trust in God will take care of the world's destiny, or that his labor to make the world inhabitable will give his existence the wholeness that can only be received in trust. The third dimension of Gogarten's view of faith, therefore, is shaped by the fact that man can only *remain* in the *perception* of himself and the world, called from nothingness into being before God, so long as he *distinguishes* the proper sphere of faith from that of works and yet does not separate them. This distinguishing is not a merely theoretical act but the most proper and highest business of faith itself, since it concerns the believer's perception of the ends to which his being and action are respectively directed.[26]

Although there are a number of questions about the relation of faith and works which need to be clarified, they must wait until the next chapter since we are primarily interested here in discovering the authentic subjectivity of faith. In sketching the dimensions of the decision of faith—perceiving, remaining, distinguishing—we have described a single phenomenon from three angles in order to show that for Gogarten the self-understanding of faith can have no antecedent on which it is based. This means that the "reality of God and His revelation has

---

[26] WIC, p. 96.

the believing man as its presupposition." [27] But how can we call such a statement anything but the rankest subjectivism? Although the subject plays the pivotal role in Gogarten's understanding of faith, we need to remember the nature of the perception involved in this self-understanding. What the subject perceives is always himself as he is reflected back on himself by the power of the divine mystery and it is, therefore, a perception of both the subject and object together, in which neither can be known apart from the other so as to be a basis for the other. "Faith," Gogarten says, "only knows of God by letting itself be taken into the use God will make of man by letting man . . . be himself before Him." [28] Thus Gogarten can take up Luther's famous statement that faith is the creator of the divinity in us, interpreting it to mean that the use into which God wants to take us is to be God "in us," i.e., *our* God. Of course faith does not create the divinity in itself but makes room for it by emptying us of the claim to be something in ourselves apart from the divine mystery. For Gogarten the meaning of Luther's statement is simply that God is honored *as God* only by faith. "For he who believes corresponds to the divinity of God, His eternal power and deity, in which He calls what is not that it may be." [29] The perception of the mystery out of which I have my being, and the perception of myself as called into being by this mystery, both happen at the same time: "God's word realizes faith, and faith lets the word be real." [30] Since the knowledge of the divine mystery comes only through the call, and since the call is only heard when one perceives himself as called into being by the mystery, the priority of the reality of God to faith can never be established outside of faith. For the mystery already involves the self in such a way that no one

[27] WG, p. 33 (Eng. tr., p. 36).
[28] *Ibid.*, p. 155 (Eng. tr., pp. 152-53).
[29] *Ibid.*, pp. 136-37 (Eng. tr., pp. 135-36).
[30] *Ibid.*, p. 18 (Eng. tr. p. 20).

can perceive the mystery without perceiving himself in it; or in more formal terms, one cannot begin to acknowledge the power of God as the Creator of the world without acknowledging himself to exist already out of this power as a creature.

What is at stake in the reality of faith, therefore, is the *being* of God and man and the world, or, more precisely, their way of *being together* in Jesus. A knowledge of this kind of object must itself be a movement of being in which neither being nor knowledge may be separated out so that one may control the other. Retrospectively, reflection may try to distinguish each element in an effort to justify the constant movement in being on the basis of knowing. But since the original and continuing movement of response to the unity of God and man in Jesus is a movement of being by which I am always reaffirming this same mode of being, the subsequent act of reflective justification would entail a movement out of the mode in which I am existing. This response to the divine mystery in the personhood of Jesus requires a constant act of repetition, or as Gogarten puts it, of remaining, and this remaining is *faith*.

The subjectivity or "interiority" of faith in Gogarten's view is unlike the subjectivity of subjectivism, however, in that it is not based on the aseity of the subject but on the call which reflects man back on himself before the mystery of existence. The subjectivity with which Gogarten is concerned is one in which

a reality encounters man that cannot by its very nature become an object and in relation to which man cannot remain his own master and grounded in himself. That is the subjectivity of personal being. In personal being a man does not stand before an object but a subject.[31]

The implication Gogarten draws is that statements of the Christian faith are only valid in the realm of this kind of sub-

[31] VJC, p. 494.

jectivity, since they "receive their particular character out of the divine call through which they are first possible and of which they speak." [32] Thus Gogarten partly affirms and partly denies the modern experience of a purely autonomous responsibility whose basis is in the subject alone. He affirms this autonomy to the extent that self-conscious responsibility for the world actually arises through faith, through the call of the divine mystery which radically reflects man back on himself. Yet Gogarten does not have this reflection originate in the subject's action—and to that extent the modern trend of autonomy is denied, but describes it as a *being reflected* back on the self by the power of the history which occurs in the Cross and Resurrection.

If we were to choose a single synonym to gather up what Gogarten means by faith it would have to be "freedom"—freedom, of course, in the sense of openness for one's destiny and therefore as courage. Faith is the twofold awareness that 1) we have shut ourselves and the world against the impenetrable mystery and stand with the world under the annihilating power of the debt of our being, and 2) that we are called with the world out of this guilt and nothingness into freedom for God. Or in Gogarten's own words, faith perceives the darkness which engulfs man and his world as the "darkness with which God covers himself when he reveals himself, the 'nothing,' therefore, through which God destroys while making alive." [33] Faith in Gogarten's view does not provide assurance in the midst of uncertainty but keeps men exposed to the unfathomable mystery of existence, to the contingency and obscurity of the future. So long as faith executes its commission, so long as man remains in the freedom into which he has been called, the world will remain open to its mysterious ground, and the powers, whatever their shape or potency, will be demystified and kept secular. Or, in traditional language, man will preserve the world as creation by perceiving the invisible presence of the Creator in all that he encounters.

So far we have tried to show how Gogarten can let faith be a free decision of the subject and yet be grounded in the reality of the object. There remain two important aspects of his concept of faith which have not been explored. First, where and how do we come into contact with the personhood of Jesus? And second, how does Gogarten relate faith's perception of the word of Jesus' historical reality to the way this history is seen by historical research?

3

Faith and Community

It is easy enough to say that the word-bound event which calls faith into being comes to us through the preaching of the church, but we would obviously miss the intention of the event if the church were thought of as the custodian of a historical report. For the preaching of the kerygma, as Gogarten points out, is not a kind of information service but a herald's (*keryx*) declaration of the will of the one who has sent him.[34] Of course information about past events may be a part of this declaration, but the messenger will speak an immediate word which announces the intention hidden in the past events of Jesus' history. The publicly visible events of Jesus' life are bound to this intention since it is only through the responsibility which Jesus fulfills through his actions that the mystery is revealed in him. Through his obedience or responsibility the visible side of his life is united with the invisible life which is grounded in the divine mystery. And this same obedience in its capacity to unite God and the world happens for us again in the kerygma. If the church is to declare what has happened and what will

[34] EK, pp. 69-70 (Eng. tr., pp. 68-69).

happen in Jesus, it must "inquire after this obedience . . . otherwise one is dealing only with the *res gestae* which cannot in any way be believed in." [35] To say that we meet the personhood of Jesus through the speech of the community means that the "person and history of Jesus are present in the *kerygma* with the same historical presence as was present with the disciples and with the community of today and the future." [36] For faith can never be directed to the kerygma in any other sense than to the mystery of God which was and is present for us in the humanity of Jesus. Gogarten describes the Word of God in the kerygma as a direct word,

> full of the most powerful intention, since it is the relation of God to the one to whom He speaks. . . . This intention is, if you will, the whole "content" of the word. This word is God himself in his relation to the one to whom the word is spoken. Thus whoever hears this word as a medium of understanding, simply does not "hear" it, but only he who surrenders himself to the intention of the One whose word it is.[37]

The actual content of the church's speech, then, is the new creation, the being out of God in Jesus of Nazareth which is hidden to the prying eye of the public. Gogarten describes the preaching of this personhood as possible only when the speaker opens himself to his hearers in his personal being which he has received from God.[38] Gogarten does not mean a kind of sharing of inner experiences but is pointing to the concreteness and actuality of the Word of God in preaching. Because the content of the Word is the presence of the divine mystery for us in the life of Jesus, it cannot be transmitted merely if talked about, but only if those who have been drawn out of their securities by the Word actually expose themselves to others in their own

[35] *Ibid.*, p. 74 (Eng. tr., p. 74).
[36] *Ibid.*, p. 75 (Eng. tr., p. 75).
[37] MZGW, p. 226.
[38] KW, p. 113.

human vulnerability. The language of Christian witness must never be a rehearsal of facts or doctrines or even a dramatic or aesthetic portrayal, but must always include a direct appeal which speaks the intention of the divine mystery in the Cross and Resurrection. Gogarten is saying that the basic problem faced by the preacher or layman is not how to communicate the Christian message—as though we knew exactly what it was and only had to figure out how to "get it across"—but is a matter of how to invite others to embark on the path of a mode of existence which is without guarantees of any kind.

A Word of this sort obviously cannot be possessed by the community; rather, the Word creates and preserves the community, so that what we are accustomed to call "church" is in fact *constituted* by speaking and hearing in the immediate personal sense. Where preaching takes place as answer, as confession to God's word, there is church, there church happens.[39] The centrality of the community's proclamation of the kerygma would seem to require an articulated doctrine of tradition. Gogarten, however, refers the church only to the biblical witness as its basis of continuity. Here again the same distinction is made between the human words of the Bible and the Word to which human words bear witness in response. Since the witnessing words of the apostolic age are a response to the single mystery of the Word of God, the latter is present in them only indirectly. To say that the biblical books were written under the inspiration of the Holy Spirit means for Gogarten that the writers' response was not determined simply by human wisdom but stood under the power of the Word. Accordingly, Gogarten delineates two aspects of the answering word in the New Testament: one which depends entirely on the mystery of Jesus' humanity, the other which is determined by the situation of the responder. The first aspect points to the answer man can give only with himself, the second to the vocabulary and

[39] *Ibid.*, p. 111.

135

style, determined by the law of his particular world, through which the New Testament writer formulates what has happened to him through the Word.[40] This dialogue between the old man under the law and the new man under grace is the concrete form in which much of the apostolic response is framed and is what Gogarten calls "theology." The proper relation of faith to the biblical words, therefore, is to treat these words as witnesses to the Word. This means that one can never take over the witness of another as his own since

genuine faith does not rest on human wisdom but the power of God, that is, on one's own hearing of God's word. For only in this hearing is the Spirit of God present and only in this hearing do I experience the power of God in which I receive myself out of God's word.[41]

4

Faith and Historical Research

The question we must try to settle here is how Gogarten relates our perception of the "intention" of God for us in the history of Jesus to the way historical research sees this history. Because modern techniques of research have their origin in the Renaissance and Enlightenment reaction against the authority of the ancient world, historical thought has been obsessed with developing techniques for separating reliable documents from forgeries and the actual chain of events from legendary accretions. What becomes of this critical attitude if our interest turns from what "really" happened in the positivistic sense to the "word" of the event in Gogarten's sense?

The concrete form of the problem here is the absence of any direct documentation for the essential dimension of Jesus' personhood, his relation to the divine mystery in all that he says

[40] MZGW, pp. 257-61.
[41] Ibid., p. 262.

and does. Speaking of the obedience or responsibility of Jesus, for example, Gogarten points out that there is no possibility of a historical (*historisch*) proof since even with the best documents the only thing we could prove is the external fact that a Messianic pretender was crucified.[42] But what is decisive for Christian faith "occurred in the obedience or the faith of the one who died on the cross." [43] Since we cannot confirm another man's faith objectively, the faith of Jesus must be perceived by faith. But this does not mean—and here Gogarten is quite insistent—that Jesus' obedience is not historical just because it slips through the net of positivistic historicism.[44] In other words, Gogarten is arguing that what happens between Jesus and God is no more superhistorical than the deepest aspect of the love of a father for his son. In the case of a human father and son our only clue will be their own testimony to this invisible aspect of their relation. This would be especially true if the public circumstances seemed to indicate that the father did not care what happened to his son even though his son continued to trust him completely. On the basis of the external evidence the father may have apparently disowned the son and perhaps even cursed him, but for those who perceive what is not apparent the story has quite another meaning.

But what is it that the believer can perceive which the researcher cannot? First of all it is the invisible power and deity of God. What the believer perceives in the Cross and Resurrection is not simply a crucifixion and "appearances" which he may reconstruct on the basis of the findings of research, but the abyss of the divine majesty into which Jesus willingly enters. trusting in the Word of God out of which he has lived and by which he has been sent. The facts—the publicly visible and demonstrable character of the event—are for Gogarten a sign

[42] WIC, p. 36.
[43] *Ibid.*
[44] *Ibid.*

pointing to the word-event between the Father and Son and the world. But in no sense, he adds, should these facts be designated the reality in which faith believes even though this reality is inseparable from the visible and measurable dimension of Jesus' history.[45] The historian *qua* research scientist does not see the reality which faith perceives due to the very nature of the preconceptual limits of his visual field. This is the direct implication of Gogarten's argument that science, by the way it structures reality in terms of strictly delimited fields and methods, excludes the question of the unity of history.

No attempt to reconstruct or interpret the history of Jesus that bypasses the intention which is preserved in Jesus' preaching and in the response of the apostolic witnesses can hope to hear what happened for faith. And because this preaching and witness are handed on through the proclamation of the community in the sense we indicated in the preceding section, Gogarten concludes that we can know the history from which Christian faith arises only through the message of the church. For this history as it is passed on in the church's kerygma does not arise from the intramundane context, and thus its pastness is not of the sort that can be looked back on in the same way we imaginatively review a past succession of events along a time continuum.[46] Since the history which gives rise to faith is the revelation of the divine mystery in the person of Jesus, it cannot be substantiated from without but can only prove its own reality by occurring again. The historical reality of the events reported in the New Testament, therefore, is not to be sought in

the "objective" and historically demonstrable fact of their having taken place, but in the *kerygma,* the witnessing proclamation that

[45] VH, p. 167. See also Gogarten's discussion of Luther's concept of the "use" God makes of the history of Jesus and the relation of this particular concept of "use" to the notion of historical fact and historical reality (ZThK, 1953, pp. 388-90).

[46] EK, p. 76 (Eng. tr., p. 77).

in the events of this history God turns with grace towards mankind and their world. If one separates the history of Jesus Christ from this proclamation in which alone it comes to us, one is losing precisely the history upon which everything depends because without it there can be no genuine, that is, justifying faith.[47]

In his recent book on Christology Gogarten further clarifies the self-authenticating character of the history which is the basis and content of the kerygma and can be known only through the kerygma.[48] He emphasizes that the faith which is able to perceive this history is one through which the man who believes is actually empowered to the same obedience which Jesus fulfilled for his sake.[49] It is not a faith, therefore, which *asserts* something to have happened, but one which *participates* in the history that is at the basis of the kerygma by recognizing in the destiny of Jesus one's own destiny as well as that of the world. Gogarten can say—in a statement reminiscent of Wilhelm Herrmann—that if a man comes to an indubitable recognition of his own existence in the Cross and Resurrection of Jesus, then there can for him be "no doubt concerning the historical (*geschichtlich*) reality as well as the true humanity of the man by whom and by whose destiny he has come to this knowledge." [50]

But must not Gogarten, who speaks so affirmatively of modern science as the legitimate expression of the Christian's freedom from the powers, allow some positive role to historical research? Despite his criticism of positivistic historicism's claim to have discovered "real" history, Gogarten has no intention of trying to set a theological limit to empirical research—which he is convinced can go its own way relatively undisturbed by

[47] *Ibid.*, pp. 44-45 (Eng. tr., pp. 37-38).
[48] JCWW, p. 67.
[49] *Ibid.*, p. 54.
[50] *Ibid.*, p. 73. Cf. Wilhelm Herrmann, *Dogmatik* (Gotha-Stuttgart, 1925), pp. 28 ff.

philosophical quarrels over the nature of historical reality and the meaning of history. That research ignores the claim of past events and does not perceive the presence of the divine mystery is not a fault to be corrected, but simply part of the preconceptual limits within which research operates. Therefore Gogarten, like Bultmann, cheerfully allows the historian to perform his critical work in which the evidence of Josephus, Tacitus, the Talmud, the apocryphal writings and archaeological artifacts, carry as much weight initially as the canonical Scripture. For he knows that *the* history which concerns faith —what happens between the Father and the Son and the world—is no more available to the archaeologist's brush than it was unambiguously apparent to everyone who saw Jesus in the flesh. For this history is not directly accessible and is in this respect like the existential movement of Kierkegaard's Knight of Faith. Certainly on questions of date, geography, the words and deeds of Jesus, the world view of the time, the historian can inform and correct the church and the theologian can only be grateful for being able to possess a clearer picture of the "facts" in this sense. As far as Gogarten is concerned, so long as research remains genuinely scientific it will perform the indispensable service of presenting the New Testament in all its strangeness to our accustomed categories.[51] An even greater benefit accruing from the application of historical criticism is the liberation of theology from the remnants of the categories of late Greek metaphysics. Although these categories retained the "profundity and truly philosophical significance of Greek thought" in the theology of the ancient church, today they are often reduced to such wretched and meager rationalizations as "objective facts." [52]

Drawing together Gogarten's scattered remarks on the subject of empirical research, we see that although he believes re-

[51] VJC, p. 37.
[52] EK, p. 114 (Eng. tr., p. 89).

search has helped to open up the path of freedom for theology, the factual product of research must be kept in perspective for what it is—an abstraction from the living reality of history which by its very nature cannot be the sole criterion of the reality of events since the quest for facts deliberately sets aside the question of significance. Facts only appear when we abstract from the concreteness of lived history certain aspects amenable to impersonal measurement or description. The "fact" that a man by the name of Jesus of Nazareth was executed as a Messianic pretender does not give us the historical reality of the crucifixion but represents an abstraction from the concrete experience of those who were present, whether they were shouting "Blasphemer!" or confessing "Truly, this was a Son of God." Therefore the historian, if he is to be more than a mere chronicler, cannot consider his work finished until he shows the possible modes of existence exhibited in the original complex which is presented to him in fragmentary witnesses of the most diverse sorts. Until he does this interpretative work, the facts are liable to be so bare and abstract as to be totally meaningless even as facts. For I cannot even know what it means that someone is crucified as a Messianic pretender unless I can understand it in terms of the general possibilities of human existence.[53] To confirm a fact is to apply predetermined measures of various sorts; to confirm a possibility, however, would mean to take the risk of living in its claim. The historian can confirm facts in the first sense, but *qua* historian he does not confirm possibilities but only exhibits them. It seems to me Gogarten makes the work of the theologian approach that of the historian who exhibits the possibilities of existence to be found in the past, although the theologian is bound to the claim of one set of possibilities so that he has the further task of showing how and where the claim of Jesus' history, as it comes to expression in the *kerygma,* collides with the claims of the present.

[53] *Ibid.,* p. 45 (Eng. tr., p. 38).

The Secularization of History

There are two questions about Gogarten's understanding of faith which need to be raised at this point. The more serious one concerns his understanding of how the reality in which faith believes is preveniently present in the believer's self-consciousness. Does this mean we can attain freedom and openness to the oncoming future apart from the history of Jesus? If the certainty of the nothingness of our being is actually the certainty of God's grace, what else is needed but to remain aware of our constantly falling back into the effort to secure our lives against the future and continually to confess the "nothingness" that comes over us in this effort? It would seem Heidegger has accounted for this dialectic of authentic and inauthentic existence in his notion of response to the call of conscience in which man accepts the guilt of his fallenness and opens himself to the future in resolve. As a matter of fact, Gogarten himself has at least once equated "being out of God" and its correlated responsibility for the world with Heidegger's "authentic existence." [54] There is no need to object to his use of Heidegger in itself, but it could be asked whether Gogarten has not given us a description of a kind of salvation by the grace of mystery which can operate on its own dynamic quite apart from the historical person of Jesus. Of course, Gogarten describes the bondage of man to nothingness as such that a man inevitably gets himself more deeply enmeshed in self-enclosure the more he tries to open himself to the mystery. But since Gogarten says that the experience of nothingness is effected in man by the mystery itself prior to faith, and that man's preparation to faith includes his freedom to let himself be put in question, it seems that all a man needs is the knowledge that his own effort to open himself is self-defeating, and that he must continually wait on the "grace of Being." This is an existential objection, however, to which only an existential answer can be given. To attempt some kind of objective demonstration—the notion of a divine plan,

[54] WG, p. 158 (Eng. tr., p. 156).

for example, according to which things are so arranged that man can only become genuinely free through Jesus—would in Gogarten's view destroy genuine faith which is based solely on the actual experience of grace. On this point Gogarten would agree with Bultmann's statement that the "only new thing that faith and faith alone is able to say about revelation is that it has become an event and becomes an event." [55]

If we turn to the problem of faith and historical research, we see that Gogarten's requirement that faith be pure faith and not based on anything outside itself results in a radical dualism between the "external" and "internal" aspects of Jesus' history which appears to immunize the personhood of Jesus from the results of research. This hardly seems the kind of freedom Gogarten says theology is supposed to receive from historical thought, especially a theology which calls its approach historical as opposed to metaphysical. And while Gogarten himself is critical of those who think they are treating revelation historically when they substitute a historical/superhistorical dichotomy for the old natural/supernatural scheme, what are we to think of his own dichotomy between the ordinary external aspect of events available to research and the invisible and internal aspect which can be perceived only by the believer? In replying to a similar question put to him by Wilhelm Kamlah, Gogarten wrote that "everything for me" depends on understanding the event of revelation as "historical in the most genuine sense." And "historical in the genuine sense" means, Gogarten continues,

that if this history is other than what we normally call history, and it obviously is, nevertheless the governing distinction here must not be of the kind that can only be described by a different concept of history, that is to say super-history. The difference must be sought within history. In exactly the same way that the difference

[55] Bultmann, *Existence and Faith*, p. 100.

143

of the man whose history with God is at stake in this event, does not consist in his being something like a superman. . . . For only so long as he is "true man" does the continuity between him and us remain without which one can no longer understand him as saviour in the sense of Christian faith. The latter understands him as saviour because it believes in him as *the* man who is one with God. What I am concerned about is the genuine historical character of this oneness in the sense I have described.[56]

When Gogarten says elsewhere that this history can only be perceived by faith, he means that because the believer comes to the history of Jesus as witnessed in the New Testament while under the pressure of the question of being or nothingness put to him by the absolute mystery, he is able to "see" this power of the divine mystery in Jesus—or in all history, for that matter. But the researcher *qua* historian must set aside the question of his own being or nothingness and ask only questions of date, location, causal connection.

Thus Gogarten, like Bultmann, is not speaking so much of two different kinds of history as he is of two ways of approaching historical reality which turn up quite different answers on the basis of different questions. But he does not really resolve the problem of the relation of these two approaches except to let each go its own way. This is no doubt because of his refusal to admit any sort of "proof" for the revelation of God in Jesus, since the divine mystery is simply unavailable to man, and the effort to make it available by a proof would be to deny the divinity of God. Yet Gogarten does not discuss the rather different question of what we could call "negative evidence," i.e., the question of whether there is *anything* research might turn up about Jesus' external history that could lead us to change our understanding of his personhood. Of course he is not denying that the research historian can inform us of the

[56] Friedrich Gogarten, "Zur Frage nach dem Ursprung des geschichtlichen Denkens," *Evangelische Theologie*, 1954, pp. 230-31.

structure of the personhood which is implied in Jesus' preaching and mode of action, but only that research can never prove that *this way of being as person was actual or fulfilled in Jesus.* But this still does not resolve the problem of whether evidence to the effect that Jesus was, for example, a Zealot who directed a band of assassins might affect our conviction that he is "God with us."

The dilemma Gogarten gets into at this point shows why Bultmann resolutely refuses to grant the "what" of Jesus' person any relevance to faith. Gogarten and Bultmann agree that the *event* of salvation is the actual address of God which calls faith into being by reference to Jesus, and as the address of God it is the same event whether it occurred on the first Easter or yesterday afternoon. But their disagreement stems from the fact that for Bultmann the important thing is that God uses a man named Jesus to forgive us, so that even the "obedience" of Jesus is not an act of the historical Jesus but a way of saying that the historical fact of his person was used "for our service" by God.[57] Believing that Bultmann has thereby failed to retain the real scandal of particularity, Gogarten insists that the obedience or responsibility of Jesus was something he actually had to carry through to the Cross. But Gogarten's attempt to demonstrate that Jesus was in fact obedient creates the following dilemma. On the one hand faith will be in jeopardy from the results of historical research since Gogarten's case for

[57] Bultmann, *Glauben und Verstehen,* I, 213. Jesus is God's *Wunder,* the one who is there for us as "the word of forgiveness spoken by God" (*ibid.,* p. 228). "For the love directed to *me*—and this alone can make me a new creature—cannot be demonstrated by historical observation. It can only be promised to me directly; and this is what is done by the proclamation" (*Existence and Faith,* p. 87). There is a passage, however, where Bultmann is interpreting Paul that sounds remarkably like Gogarten and does not seem consistent with his strictures against the "new quest." "God raised him to be Lord who was nothing on his own account and knew no desire for recognition, and whom self-surrender and love brought to the cross, and so God has set the law of the cross over the world." (*Essays,* p. 173; I am indebted to James Goss of Cornell College for this reference.)

Jesus' obedience rests in part on the "fact" that Jesus uttered certain statements and associated with sinners. If neither of these facts were true but instead we turned up evidence which suggested, let us say, that he was crucified as the leader of an anti-Roman uprising, what would happen to our faith which is based on his? On the other hand Gogarten could avoid this horn of the dilemma by refusing to allow the external and publicly visible action of Jesus to serve as an indication of his obedience or disobedience. But this would make it possible that Jesus might have externally been guilty of disregard for his concrete neighbors or have cursed God and nevertheless in his hidden being lived in defenseless openness to God and his neighbors. One would then have to ask if this would not so radically separate being and action, or the "personal" world and the "existing" world, that the obedience of Jesus could hardly be called historical.

Bultmann's view neatly avoids this dilemma, but he pays a heavy price. Gogarten's position by contrast has the virtue of taking the concrete historical reality of Jesus' obedience seriously. And so long as we are not actually faced with strong negative evidence which might suggest that Jesus did try to legitimate his preaching or that his association with sinners was invented by the early community, Gogarten's account of how faith comes to its certainty about the historical reality of Jesus does avoid the twin pitfalls of either seeking a historical proof for faith or of turning faith into mere assertions. For it is clear that Gogarten believes faith can only testify to Jesus' obedience because Jesus' own proclamation and the proclamation of the church in which this faith and obedience has come to expression are able to call forth the same faith and obedience in others. The issue, therefore, is not whether Jesus' obedience or responsibility was "perfect," but whether the *kerygma* which announces its significance has the power to open us for the future.

V

SECULAR ETHICS

1

The Risk of Reason

The secularization of ethics has meant a shift from a world whose social and political order was divinely given to a world of purely human and historical norms. In both the ancient world and the Middle Ages man sought the given structures of reality before which he was held accountable, but now the normative arrangements and sanctions are believed to be fashioned by man himself who is responsible only to his own conscience. Thanks to the fantastic pace of scientific and technological development, the historical transformation of norms runs faster and faster. Although the disorientation

147

brought about by this rapid tempo of change has increasingly led many to lament a breakdown of morality, Gogarten thinks our period is as morally earnest as any since man simply cannot live without some kind of coherence and order, however minimal. There can be no doubt, for example, that among the virtues of our technological societies are the discipline, industriousness, and alertness essential to coordinate an increasingly complex assemblage of machines, and an enormously intricate social and economic structure. The fundamental principle of coherence underlying all these virtues is the responsibility for the form of the world placed on man by his freedom from the cosmic powers. Now the noble aim of this responsibility is the administration of the world for the welfare of man, but, ironically, the more this ethos succeeds in organizing the world, the less room there seems for man as a person since he increasingly becomes a piece of the apparatus needed to keep things functioning smoothly.[1] Here is where Gogarten sees the great danger in the secular ethos—not in technology as such but in the tendency of a totally subject-centered responsibility to ignore the mystery of the world and of human existence and to honor no bond or obligation which might limit man's action.[2] Nevertheless, man's life must be bound together by something if it is to be human. Therefore, so long as he refuses the primordial bond in which his existence as man is grounded in his relation to God and neighbor, he must seek the coherence of his life elsewhere. As a result, secular man is constantly tempted to find a bond for his life within the world—in race or religion or political ideology or simply in his own inner drive to remain autonomous. But when this happens he makes himself and others subject to this "law" which then becomes the end justifying any means. Legitimately alarmed at the continuing propensity of modern man for totalitarian solutions to the

[1] WIC, p. 58.
[2] MZGW, pp. 372-73, 380-81.

problem of order, some have called for the stabilizing force of a revealed or natural law ethic which would protect the integrity of personal existence. Gogarten believes this kind of solution is untenable since we cannot return to a supernaturally ordered cosmos. The only kind of bond that is possible for secular man is an obligation he experiences in his self-consciousness.[3]

Not surprisingly, Gogarten concludes that the answer to the destruction of personal life and the dissolution of the fundamental orders of society through technological bureaucracy is not a Christian ethic which would bind man from without, but the kind of existence in faith in which a man is ready for the divine mystery and thereby for the mystery of his own and his neighbor's humanity. To grasp the ethical significance of such a faith, it is necessary to keep in mind the two dimensions of the Christian's responsibility for the world: the dimension of faith and the dimension of works. Faith, Gogarten says, is directed to the "invisible and protects the divine reality of salvation in that it gives God the honor and in its emptiness is filled with the assurance that what God promises he is powerful to do." [4] Works are directed exclusively to what he is able to accomplish in terms of the proximate ends he seeks to achieve. Taken together, faith and works form a single responsibility so long as the works are done in the context of freedom from the law and thereby correspond to faith.[5] If the two dimensions of responsibility were connected from the other direction so that works were in some sense necessary for the full realization of faith, God would be robbed of his divinity through man's effort to foreclose the future. Gogarten's way of uniting faith and works, therefore, is to give each a complementary but clearly distinguishable task:

[3] VJC, pp. 459-63.
[4] WIC, p. 85.
[5] Ibid.

Over against the world man is independent . . . he lives out of his works. Over against God he is . . . purely a receiver, he lives out of grace alone. Both are valid for the same life. . . . For there is only one life that man lives in the world before God. And it is the same man, who does not belong partly to one and partly to the other, but belongs entirely to both. Thus he must be both at the same time: wholly independent and wholly receiving, living wholly out of works and wholly out of grace.[6]

In order to grasp the full import of Gogarten's notion of the relation between faith and works, however, we also need to recall the pivotal role he gives to Paul's "all is permitted." This phrase embodies the essence of Christian responsibility since it expresses man's radical freedom from all cosmic powers. Another way of putting it is to say that the power of the law is now seen as a creaturely power that is turned over to man. Yet this custody of the law is not license since the law is not left to mere whim but to the test of reason. Justification by faith means that *all* man's actions fall into this realm of testing, and for that reason the decision of faith is at stake in every action of his daily life since he is constantly called upon to distinguish faith and works.[7]

Gogarten concludes, therefore, that faith cannot and must not try to provide principles by which to determine "what" works are to be done. When the world is turned over to man, he alone is responsible for the content of his decisions. There are two reasons for this, both of which follow from Gogarten's notion of the personal character of man's relation to God. First, the personhood of man in faith cannot depend directly on his particular actions in the world but only on his response to God and his fellowmen. This response must not be determined by any of the structures or laws of the world since this would allow the creature to determine his relation to the Creator. But do

[6] VJC, p. 17.
[7] VH, pp. 95-96.

not our actions taken as a whole constitute our relationships or, at the very least, decisively modify their character? Gogarten denies this in respect of man's relation to God. According to his distinction between the active and receptive dimensions of man's nature, no amount of action in the world can make a man a receiver before the divine mystery. Here Gogarten is following Luther who says that being precedes doing, and suffering (in the sense of receiving) precedes being.[8] Gogarten never tires of repeating that what is involved in man's relation to God (and to his neighbor in God) is being and not doing since the presence of God in the personhood of Jesus does not demand first of all an action in terms of the world and its structures but a response with oneself.[9]

The second factor which keeps faith from becoming a source of ethical principles is man's responsibility for ordering the world through his rationally directed action. Since the rational capacity for controlling what is beneath him is the same he possessed before coming into faith, and since faith has merely liberated him from seeking his being in the fruits of this action, faith could not determine the content of the Christian's works without contradicting itself. The requirement of some kind of Christian ethic would change his relation to God from one of total and unconditional receptivity to one which is determined by his ethical action. Then God would not be honored as the Creator in whom alone man has his being, but would be reduced to the status of one of the many divinities of the world which man tries to satisfy through special ethical or sacramental actions.[10]

[8] *Ibid.*, p. 219.
[9] *Ibid.*, p. 217.
[10] Luther's concept of the "all working" character of God is behind Gogarten's thinking here. As he sees it, the great insight that made Luther a reformer was that man's personhood must be grounded solely in the power of God and cannot depend on his moral action lest God be robbed of his majesty and man fail his genuine personal being (ZThK, 1950, pp. 228-30, 264).

The Secularization of History

Does faith have no effect at all on works? Only in the sense of "how" a man understands the relation of works to his destiny as a whole. By circumscribing the realm of works as a whole and sharply distinguishing this dimension of existence from itself, faith exposes man's works to the mystery of the future and changes them from works meant to secure man's existence into works which aim only at preparing for that part of the future which lies in man's control. Thereby the freedom for the divine mystery which a man receives in faith provides a bond for human life which limits man's activity to purely worldly and proximate ends. Within this boundary, however, man is ethically autonomous.[11] Although the necessity of order is built into the nature of things, what *forms* this order must take from time to time is the task turned over to man to be fulfilled through the risk of reason.[12] Thus when the fundamental bond which grounds man's being in his relation to God and the neighbor is perceived and preserved, the same man who recognizes himself as his own master can also recognize himself as a creature of God and the order and coherence he seeks for his world as the creation of God.[13]

There is always the risk that man will misuse his maturity and fail to rise to the challenge of his responsibility. Some think the "risk of reason" is too great and believe there must be an external law imposed on man's reason; yet for Gogarten, such a surrender of autonomy and independence would be to surrender man's sonship and miss the freedom of faith. The venture of reason always takes place for the Christian within the context of the venture of faith, or, as

[11] VH, p. 218.
[12] Gogarten, *Das Bekenntnis der Kirche* (Jena, 1934), p. 30. One must be careful in using Gogarten's politically oriented writing of 1928-37 to illuminate his postwar works, since there is an important shift in the later writing in his understanding of secularization and independence as well as a repudiation of the *Volk* idea (*Die Kirche in der Welt*, pp. 9-22). See also Appendix.
[13] MZGW, p. 211.

Gogarten wrote many years ago, "it is through the risk of reason that our earthly life becomes historical and reason leads us before the risk of faith along many paths, paths we cannot see in advance." [14]

It is striking that in Gogarten's writings since 1952 the "neighbor" who plays a central role in all the earlier works is seldom encountered even in discussions of ethics. Although the works published in the 1950's are still dominated by the motif of personhood, the impression we get from these writings is one of the man of faith standing alone before God with the burden of his responsibility for the world. Nevertheless, the continuity between the two periods is there despite the fact that Gogarten has made little effort to clarify the exact role man's relation to his neighbor plays in responsibility for the world.

The key to the continuity between the apparently impersonal responsibility for the world and the love for the neighbor is found in Gogarten's understanding of the inseparability of freedom for the future of God and freedom to serve the neighbor's need. The basis for the unity of the God-man and man-man relationship is that both are equally primordial. We have seen in the earlier discussion of personhood that the bond which links man and man is not added to human nature any more than is man's relation to God. Genuine ethical freedom is not a freedom "from" others as though man were self-contained and subsequently might decide to establish a relation to his fellowmen, but a freedom "for" others within the bond that already exists.

The love or freedom for the neighbor which becomes possible in faith, therefore, is no more to be achieved by action than faith itself, since to love means in this case to belong to another in the freedom of reciprocity, a receiving in giving and a

[14] Gogarten, *Das Bekenntnis der Kirche*, p. 30.

giving in receiving.[15] In *Politische Ethik,* Gogarten defined love as "being-for-the-other" in the same way in which I have my "being-from-him." Genuine love, therefore, occurs only where man's "being-for-the-other" and his "being-from-the-other" are *both* present. If he is only *for* the other, he loves as a duty. If his love is determined only by what comes *from* the other, he experiences a causal and erotic love.[16] It follows that no one can make himself free to love but will love only to the extent he has received himself in love. Genuine love—as seen in Jesus' command to love the enemy—does not look at the character or worth of the other but opens itself to the person. But such a love is impossible for the man who *tries* to love, since his effort shuts him tighter in the circle of self-realization. We can only love, Gogarten concludes, in the confession of our impotence to love.[17] In this way our relation to one another is the place where being and nothingness are experienced before the mystery of existence since we cannot believe in God while bypassing the reality in which we live.[18] But our reality as man

is in the call of the neighbor and our responsibility before this call. Whether we believe in God is decided by whether or not we hear and answer this call. . . . But this call can only be heard and answered when I hear the brother, the neighbor who calls, . . . who does not seek this or that, but myself. . . . When that happens I receive my reality as God gives it to me in this man, and confess Him in this hearing and answering as my Lord.[19]

Nevertheless, even though love does not lie in our power, it is still commanded. This is true because love, trust, fidelity belong to the nature of man. Gogarten rejects the idea that love or fidelity are supernatural gifts since, "if man is to be man, he must love." [20] The command to love remains, therefore, not

[15] VJC, p. 511.
[16] Gogarten, *Politische Ethik,* pp. 100-1.
[17] VJC, pp. 512-13.
[18] *Ibid.,* p. 513.
[19] *Ibid.*   [20] *Ibid.,* p. 514.

as something "one does" if he is a Christian, but as a "thou shalt" which reveals my indebtedness before God and other men. Even as the command demands that I open myself to others, it reveals that my very effort to love only shuts me against them. The command to love cannot be withdrawn from this contradiction—that I must try to do something that I know I cannot, and that my very attempt forces me to do what I do not want, to cut myself off from God and man. (Rom. 7:15.) There is freedom from this duplicity only in a faith which knows that the command cannot be fulfilled because it demands man himself. The faith that knows this also believes in Christ in whom the command of love judges the guilty and inverted existence of man and offers its most powerful healing since what is revealed to the believer

in the cross of Jesus Christ is his own reality. But it is revealed in the face of a love that opens itself to *him,* the surd one (*dem Nichtigen*). This is the other thing revealed to him: the love of God, that has appeared in God sending his only begotten Son that we should have life through him. (John 4:10.) In this love, in the sending of Jesus Christ, a man encounters him who becomes his neighbor. That which we wanted others to do and which we owed to them and still owe he does to us. Here love is not demanded, it occurs before our own love.[21]

The command to love is the reminder of God's love which is present for us in the Word of God, the man Jesus. But this command does not come to the man of faith as something he thinks he can fulfill by his own efforts. Rather, it comes as the reminder that every man is his neighbor and that, even though he is never open to all men, he owes himself to them. In this confession he remains in the love God sends and this is the fundamental determinant of his relation to others. He remains in the love God sends so long as his relation to others "explicitly or silently points to Jesus Christ and the love

[21] *Ibid.,* pp. 516-17.

of God which became powerful among us through him." [22]

Gogarten connects this love of the neighbor with the responsibility for the structures of the world through his notion of the indissoluble unity of openness to God and openness to other men. By giving man the freedom and courage to be open, faith restores him to the fundamental *bond* with God and the neighbor which constitutes his genuine personhood as creature. This bond, like the divine mystery itself, is inviolable and absolute and therefore relativizes all other bonds whether of class, race, nationality, political or religious ideology. All man's efforts to organize his world and plan for the future must aim first at preserving his being as person—rather than at technical efficiency, the smooth functioning of the state, the honor of the nation, the preservation of the church. Specifically, this means that all structures and forms that are developed in the legitimate exercise of responsibility for the world—even where this concerns the machinery of commerce and industry—must "leave room for the personal being of those who are related to each other in them." [23] If we take this kind of precaution in our planning and building, the structures we shape can participate in the inviolability of man's personhood. Of course there is no way we could guarantee the personhood of man since it must always be laid hold of anew in the freedom of faith. But so long as man "remains in respon-

---

[22] *Ibid.*, p. 520. Gogarten cites here and throughout his discussion Kierkegaard's *Works of Love*. An earlier chapter in *Die Verkündigung Jesu Christi* is also devoted to Christ's command to love. There he emphasizes that Jesus' command to love means that the reality of God is revealed in the relations of men to each other; but it is revealed there in its true intention—as love—only in Christ. "The reality of God . . . is present in every man who is dependent on our mercy and help. And whether a man is open to God's freely given goodness and lives by trust in Him . . . is unfailingly seen in whether he is ready to open himself to the neighbor despite the structures of the world. Thus faith in God and love to the neighbor are intimately bound to each other. Both concern the same reality" (p. 112).

[23] *Ibid.*, p. 540.

sibility before the on-coming future . . . where he exposes himself to his futurity, there he can use the most powerful and complicated technological apparatus without losing himself in it." [24]

Although "responsibility for the world" in Gogarten's postwar writings sometimes gives the impression of an abstractness similar to the Kantian categorical imperative, his writings of the late 1920's attempted to express responsibility concretely in terms of Luther's concept of "office" or "position" (*Stand*).[25] The insistence of Gibson Winter and Harvey Cox that the impersonality of human relationships in the urban setting is not only necessary for the functioning of the city but also for the preservation of human integrity suggests the relevance of this Lutheran notion for the "secular city." [26] As Gogarten pointed out in his earlier work, responsibility is not just a general principle but the responsibility of a father, bus-driver, teacher, artist, voter, etc. And so long as a man fulfills the responsibilities of the various positions he occupies, he does works of love—whether he experiences feelings of love or not. The basic structures we have developed in our social and political life are not there for the private use and profit of the individuals who exercise the positions within them, but for the reciprocal benefit of those on both the receiving and giving end.[27] Of course a man may misuse his position for personal

[24] MZGW, p. 424.
[25] Gogarten, *Die Schuld der Kirche gegen die Welt* (Jena, 1930, 2nd ed. [1st ed., 1928]). In the Foreword to the second edition he emphasized that the positions (*Stände*) receive their historical form through man's reason, but as part of creation they are related to man's being. The chief aim of the work was to underline that man has his being "from-the-other" in the concrete situation (pp. 8-10).
[26] Gibson Winter, *The Suburban Captivity of the Churches* (New York, 1961,) pp. 30 ff. See also Winter's *The New Creation as Metropolis* (New York, 1963). Cox is particularly emphatic on this point and suggests that we need to evolve a conceptuality for appreciating the "I-you" relationship (*The Secular City* [New York, 1965], pp. 48-49).
[27] Gogarten, *Die Schuld der Kirche gegen die Welt,* pp. 39-40.

gain or as an opportunity to vent his prejudice or satisfy his psychic needs at the expense of others, but then he is no longer acting in the capacity of his position but as a private person. When this happens, he is in danger of forfeiting his own humanity and injuring the humanity of all by corroding the structures we have developed to make communal life possible.[28]

The difficulty with the "position" concept is that it can so easily be misunderstood in a conservative or reactionary sense —and this misunderstanding (although not without some basis) greeted Gogarten's earlier use of it.[29] In the light of this misapprehension it is perhaps worth stressing again that Gogarten's concept of responsibility does not primarily bear the middle-class connotation which clings to a phrase like "he is a responsible person," but refers to the primordial structure of man's being from others and being for others. Genuine responsibility, therefore, is rooted in the response which the presence of another man demands, a response which is given by being present for him in return. Even in his earlier work, Gogarten stressed that care for the political order which arises from this responsibility entails a continual reforming of the "positions," especially since modern technology has meant the constantly accelerating change in old social structures and the rise of new ones.[30] Once the concept of the positions is set in the context of secularization, it loses the last vestiges of a conservative or middle-class tendency. Basically, the concept means that our relation to others nearly always

[28] *Ibid.,* pp. 40-41.

[29] In the *Politische Ethik,* Gogarten says that in his writings of this period he wants to revive Luther's claim that man pleases God when he serves him in his position and not in self-chosen works. This does not mean a direct application of Luther's historically conditioned concept of society, or a conservation of the "old" order. The "positions" themselves change through man's responsibility (pp. 166-67).

[30] At the time of the *Politische Ethik* (1932) Gogarten saw the rise of the industrial working class as such a need. He attributed the political unrest of Europe to the fact that the worker had not received justice (pp. 203-4).

involves some structure, even if it is that of a tiny "sub-culture." Whether it is a neighborhood organization fighting the city planners, or an ephemeral coffee-house discussion group, or even a matter of giving street directions to a stranger, the responsibility called forth is never *merely* individual, situational, and momentary—it always has a form. Even the practice of "art for art's sake," for example, involves responsibility for a historical tradition and a contemporary community.

Seen in this light, Gogarten's concept of responsibility ceases to appear as an abstract principle and becomes a reflection of the concrete historical demands of our particular tasks in society. To be open to the neighbor is not only to be ready for personal encounters despite the barriers of the social and economic structure, but also to exercise our responsibility through these same structures insofar as they sustain the whole political order. Although reason autonomously seeks the kind of structures which accord with the nature of man as person, it perceives that the being of man and the world are mysterious and unfathomable. Because the Christian recognizes the fundamental mystery of man, he knows that technology and the state are made for man and not man for the state. Nevertheless the Christian does not have any better insight into how to organize the polis within these limits; he is directed to the "risk of reason." The Christian must devote himself to the concrete tasks of the historical present in the knowledge and expectation of the final judgment. He is not willing to sacrifice justice in the present for a supposedly perfectible future. Although he does not exclude progress in any area, he does rule out the dream of a socially or politically engineered utopia or the chaos of an idealistic or nihilistic anarchy.

For Gogarten, then, there is no such thing as a "Christian" ethic since the Christian takes the risk of reason by joining in the common task of discovering and forming the structures of the world on the basis of historical experience, rational insight,

159

and the new conditions presented by technological and social change. What does this radically secular view of ethics do to the passion for putting the church into the leadership of social change? It would certainly seem to imply that the long-standing effort to get the churches to provide "Christian" positions on the concrete social and political questions of the day has been misguided. What relation, then, *does* the church have to the world in Gogarten's view?

2

The Church and the World

In order to understand the relation of church and world in Gogarten's thought, we will need to define his concept of church more closely. As was indicated in the previous chapter, Gogarten names "church" the community of persons which exists through the speaking and hearing of the word. Those who belong to this community are not members of an organization or a mystical entity but are bound to one another by their having been called into "being out of God." Gogarten uses the "body of Christ" motif but interprets it to mean that just as Jesus is fully man yet has the basic source of his life from the power of the divine mystery, so the church is completely in the world yet does not derive its life from the structures and powers of the world.[31] Gogarten also links the statement in Eph. 4:15, that Christ is the head of the body, with the image of Christ as the one in whom "all things hold together" in Col. 1:17. The church as the body of Christ is itself all things; it is neither a separate race nor a separate place. It is not in the world as a self-contained entity but as a leaven. The church, Gogarten holds, *is* the world insofar as the world has found its head in Christ.[32]

[31] KW, pp. 81-82.
[32] *Ibid.,* p. 54.

Nevertheless Gogarten does not regard it as simply accidental that this body of Christ is a visible human community which takes on institutional forms similar to other kinds of human community. Naturally, the church will claim to be of a fundamentally different nature than other communities, yet as soon as it tries to prove its claim to be different, it makes itself "in fact into a society of the same kind as the others." [33] The only way the church can "prove" itself is to remain what it is: the community that exists in hearing, speaking, and "doing" the divine Word, and that means it must be constantly vigilant that human words and commandments not take the place of the divine Word. To preserve the purity of the gospel necessitates special organs such as doctrine, liturgy, hierarchy, which have grown more and more complex throughout the history of the church. Yet a dangerous temptation arises out of this work since right doctrine or right ethics can become a badge the church uses to distinguish itself from other institutions. But to use the Word of God in this way is to turn it into a worldly law. The church then judges its faithfulness to God by whether or not it lives up to this law. No matter how orthodox the statements of such a confession or theology, when used as a law, Gogarten believes they pervert the Word of God into an instrument to rule and guide the world. When this happens, men will not hear the gospel which brings freedom from the fateful entanglement of the real law under whose power they are living, but only an anachronistic "religious" institution claiming hegemony over men's moral and spiritual life.[34]

For Gogarten, the Word of God is not a law by which to guide ethical decision, nor is it simply the message of forgiveness (which would be "cheap grace"). The Word is both law and gospel, not one before the other but both together as gift

[33] *Ibid.*, p. 151.
[34] *Ibid.*, pp. 154-57.

and demand.[35] The law function of the Word is the same for the church as it is for the world—to reveal sin, which is the world's determination to remain enclosed in itself and oblivious of the mystery. The church is that part of the self-enclosed world which is learning to perceive the divine mystery which permeates and surrounds the world. By listening to the word of the history of Jesus, the part of the world that is the church understands that it has closed itself against the mystery.[36]

To ask of the church a more perfect set of laws by which to administer the world, therefore, would be to contradict its nature as community. The world *has* a law today, the law of freedom and responsibility. Nor does the world need the church to tell it that it has not lived up to this law, that it has been irresponsible. The world knows only too well that men have been murdered and enslaved in the name of freedom itself. The world is acutely sensitive to the fact that its very survival depends on responsible action by its political and military leaders and that irrationality or fanaticism could lead us to the brink. Modern man's responsibility for the world is experienced *as law,* as his task. He knows he ought to practice works of love toward all men, that he ought to work for peace with justice, that he should cultivate accuracy, patience, honesty, etc. He does not need the church to tell him about these virtues or to remind him he is not living up to them.[37]

What the world does not know, according to Gogarten, and what it does not want to hear from the church or anyone else, is that the enslavement and destruction of man results from the fact that its law "grasps too high." [38] Because the world tries to give itself a final meaning through its law, the law ceases to be secular and becomes a politically, metaphysically,

[35] *Ibid.,* p. 165.
[36] *Ibid.,* pp. 173-75.
[37] MZGW, p. 281.
[38] *Ibid.*

or religiously experienced absolute. The church, therefore, should teach the world two things: it should keep the world in the knowledge that it is only the world, and at the same time it should keep it in the knowledge that it is God's creation which he has reconciled to himself through Christ. To remind the world that it is "only the world," Gogarten says, is to keep the world secular, to deliver man from the anxiety-ridden attempt to justify his existence through the works of responsibility. This is simply the reverse side of the knowledge that the world is God's creation, that its meaning and wholeness are not found in itself but in God. Of course this wholeness of the world is invisible since it is the "eternal power and deity" of God himself, the unfathomable mystery which surrounds man's existence.[39]

In relation to its own life, therefore, the church's preaching reminds her that she lives only from the gospel, that her community is invisible and inaccessible. As the church of those who are neither Greek nor Jew, slave nor free, male nor female, it cannot be "found" in the world because man's relation to God cannot be seen.[40] Nonetheless, this hidden community never ceases to be externally part of the world and to live under its law. Naturally, there are those within and without the institutional church who would like to have this community sanctify the historical forms of the world's order. But no sooner does the church succumb to this temptation, than movements of resistance break out from within which sabotage her achievement. Thus the church is always what Luther called *perpetua ruina*—the world looks to it as the cement of society, but the church itself is always falling apart from within. If its attempts to become a human institution like others were not always being ruined, it would cease to be the church. From Gogarten's point of view, if the dream of reconciling and inte-

[39] *Ibid.*, pp. 283-84.
[40] *Ibid.*, pp. 286-87.

grating the church with culture were to come true, it would mean the end of the church. In a restored Christendom, in a "Christian society," the church could be influential, respectable, "relevant," in short, the inspirer, sustainer, and integrator of culture—but it would not be the church.[41]

The Church, then, is neither the political and moral tutor of the world, nor is it a world-forsaking "holy community." It is not simply "in" the world, but even as the community of the Word it has the utmost solidarity with the world. It is not a circumscribed society of those who are responsible for the world because they possess a knowledge inaccessible to others, but it is that part of the world which has found the ground of responsibility in response to God and the neighbor through Jesus Christ. This community is the church of the purest inwardness and worldlessness and at the same time of the most urgent worldliness and most intensive moral-political responsibility.[42] Since it has no secret pipeline to a revealed or natural law so that it could step in where it decides secular men have failed, the church points to the one thing it does know, to *the* boundary, *the* mystery which directs reason to the risk of caring for the world.

If the Christian community is to fulfill its task of restricting reason to its secular goals by keeping it sensitive for the mystery of existence, it must be able to distinguish the realm where the word of God rules through faith from the realm where man rules through reason. In relation to the church's message this means the community must be able to distinguish *Christianity* from *Christian faith*. As we saw earlier, Christianity for Gogarten is a secularized and moralized version of the responsibility for the world opened up by Christian faith. The essence of Christianity, therefore, is Christian ethics. From the perspective of Gogarten's understanding of the relation of church

[41] *Ibid.*, pp. 288-89.
[42] *Ibid.*, p. 276.

and world it is evident that the fault of Christianity is that it treats faith as an answer to the problem of order and to the question of the meaning of history. By thus identifying Christian faith with itself, Christianity turns faith into an ideology on the same level as others. Genuine Christian faith, however, has no answer to the question of order and history but remains in the condition of listening to the divine answer, i.e., to an answer which is impenetrable and incomprehensible to man since it is the presence of the mystery itself. By its posture of expectation before the impenetrable future, faith preserves the presence of the divine mystery with the world and restricts man's answers to their merely proximate range.[43] Gogarten goes on to point out that the confusion of Christianity with Christian faith has not only robbed faith of its openness to the future and thus muffled its genuine historicity, but it has also perverted Christianity itself. As an ethical tradition which expresses man's responsibility for the world, the phenomenon of Christianity need not be shoved aside so long as it does not become an ideology. Unlike those enthusiasts who turn the distinction between religion and Christian faith into an absolute separation, Gogarten does not despise this all too human tradition we call Christianity but believes it is worthy of our respect and cultivation so long as it is restricted to the secular level and does not become a condition of justification.[44]

3

Secularization, Secularism, and Fate

Gogarten's reply to the question of how secularization and Christian faith are related finally comes down to this: Christian faith is not only compatible with secularization but positively demands its continuance and expansion into all areas

[43] VH, pp. 198-199.
[44] *Ibid.*, pp. 223-24.

of life in order that faith can remain genuine faith. There are two requirements if secularization is to be preserved and enhanced. First, the world must remain subject to man's rational administration and man must remain free of any limits imposed from outside his own conscience. Secondly, this responsibility itself must not be permitted to become a law which poses as the final justification of man's being and action, but it must be united with an awareness of the mystery of the being of man and the world. If either of these requirements is missing, if man thinks he has a final answer to the meaning of existence or, if he gives up seeking an answer altogether, secularization has been replaced by what Gogarten calls "secularism." [45]

In one of his major postwar works Gogarten applies this secularization-secularism continuum to three phenomena which dominate much of our discussion of the contemporary situation: science, culture, and history.[46] Since the question of history is at the center of this exposition of Gogarten's thought, it would be well to look briefly at the way the secularization-secularism pattern is applied to the meaning of history. We will see that Gogarten finds the pattern finally inadequate to the deepest opposition between Christian faith and the subject-centered orientation of modern man.

Once the world has been turned over to man's responsibility through his liberation from cosmic bondage, this independence can be perpetuated apart from faith. When separated from faith, responsibility can take two directions. One is secularism which we have already mentioned. The other direction is characterized by a refusal to flee into ideology or nihilism and the willingness to remain with the ambiguities of history. Here the future remains open and the question of the unity and meaning of history is continually preserved but never resolved.

[45] *Ibid.*, pp. 146-47.
[46] MZGW, pp. 291-442.

Having avoided the pitfalls of ideology on the one side and nihilism on the other, this genuinely secular stance is nevertheless plagued by one last temptation—the temptation to absolutize its very secularity, to become so absorbed in what is proximately achievable that it grows deaf to the mystery of existence. Although the greatest virtue of science, technology, and the state is their "godlessness," it is just at the point where they become most godless that men are tempted to make secularity itself into an ideology (and therefore "secularism") by ignoring the final mystery of man's life.[47] Even here the task of faith is not to criticize modern culture for being secular but to help it fight off this temptation and preserve history for the sphere of secularization.[48]

This second direction which can be taken by responsibility apart from faith is obviously close to Christian faith itself. What is the difference, then, between this genuinely secular secularity and Christian secularity? Gogarten tries to answer this question by distinguishing between meeting the mystery of the future as *fate* and meeting it as *history*. Man experiences the future as *fate* when he cannot bear to expose himself openly and pliantly to its threat but hardens himself against it in the social-political structures and cultural forms he has already achieved. But man experiences this same mystery as *history* when he exposes himself and all his works to the future without reservation.[49] Since it is the same mystery in both cases, the freedom and courage of genuinely historical existence always bear within themselves the possibility of tragically shattering against the future. The test put to man by the imminent futurity of existence, therefore, is whether he can maintain the unity of autonomous responsibility with a perception of the divine mystery.[50]

[47] *Ibid.,* p. 380.
[48] ZThK, 1954, p. 357.
[49] MZGW, pp. 389-91.
[50] *Ibid.,* p. 393.

Gogarten points out that the Greeks could find the measure for the unity of autonomy and dependence in the divine cosmic order whose boundaries destroyed those who strayed across them. But secular man—who has lost the medieval counterpart of the Greek cosmic order—must find the boundary between autonomy and dependence within himself, in the very independence which drives him to overstep it. Whether he grasps his historicity or is crushed by it is decided by the way he understands the coherence he achieves for life through his acts of personal and corporate responsibility.[51] The alternative to clutching at the coherence he has achieved is the courage of faith which perceives the darkness of the oncoming future as the mystery of God who makes alive the dead. In both the tragic assertion which characterizes an existence in fate and in the courage and freedom of faith, man's existence is exposed to the future, and in both, his understanding of his independence is in question. The difference is in the way man holds himself before the mystery which approaches him. "In the case of faith he exposes himself to the future without any reservation of the independence he has gained through his anticipatory planning. In fate he exposes himself in the tragic and frustrated assertion of his independence." [52] Thus the *final* alternative before modern man is not secularization or secularism, but whether secular man will experience his existence in tragic refusal or in the openness and courage of faith.

Whether this faith is understood as the one which alone justifies, will be shown in its capacity to preserve man's independence toward the world. . . . If this independence and responsibility are preserved . . . then it can no longer happen that the responsibility which is given man for life turns out to be death. For he will not try to perform by works the responsibility which can only

---

[51] *Ibid.,* p. 394.
[52] *Ibid.,* p. 433.

be fulfilled in faith. The world will then be delivered from the dreadful illusion that it will only have a meaning when man gives it one. In this way the power will be taken from the fateful entanglement of subjectivism.[53]

Since Gogarten's "ethic" does not give advice about what to do but only directs the Christian to his concrete secular responsibilities, the result seems to be a radical contextualism. A strictly contextualist ethic refuses fixed principles or standards with their attendant casuistry; the individual must do whatever lies at hand in the particular situation. The ethical question is not whether we are doing the right thing but—no matter what we may be doing—whether we are acting as men of faith. Since we must take the risk of reason in the concrete case, to seek a "Christian" law in the Bible or a system of creation orders or an eternal natural law would be to forfeit the maturity we have received in Christ. For once Christian faith has freed man from the religious power of the "elemental spirits,"

there can no longer be anything to restrict him in the sense in which the pre-Christian mythical world did. But a "natural law" would be such a restriction, *before* which he would have to be responsible.[54]

Nevertheless Gogarten believes the most important question for man remains "what should be and always is"—although for modern man this can no longer mean the search for a Platonic archetype.[55]

Over against his apparent contextualism we must place Gogarten's persistent concern to discover the primordial bond which defines man's humanity. In his postwar writings, he still speaks on occasion of "orders" in a way that indicates he

[53] WG, p. 193 (Eng. tr., p. 189).
[54] *Ibid.*, p. 179 (Eng. tr., p. 176).
[55] *Ibid.*

does not believe the risk of reason simply prescribes a course of action relative to the situation, but rather that it *discovers* "boundaries" which make a genuinely human life possible. In his prewar writings Gogarten included among these orders the basic structures of sexual polarity, family, political community, judiciary, etc. The particular form of these "natural" structures depends on the historical circumstances, yet this relativism of the concrete form does not relativize the boundaries that are already there.[56] Not "already there" in the sense of constant, abstract principles to be read directly off the cosmic process, but as always embodied in a concrete form and determinate situation. Even in his prewar writings Gogarten did not conceive of the discovery of the orders of life through the risk of reason as a movement from the passing stream of history to a static suprahistorical realm but as a movement within history.

But even though Gogarten has wanted to avoid a radical contextualism, the chief feature of his postwar ethical thought remains its secularity; the decisions are the purely empirical and historical work of the autonomous reason. The question which immediately comes to mind is whether Paul's "all is permitted" really means that from the standpoint of faith all works are neutral. Is the Christian *qua* Christian actually reduced to silence in the area of ethics, so that he can only

[56] Gogarten's rejection of natural law is based on the continental tradition which sees natural law as a body of static principles. Yet Gogarten himself has spoken of "natural" orders. He once wrote, for example, that "it is not the task of the redeemed man . . . to 'Christianize' the world. . . . But what does matter is the knowledge of the orders of the world in their simple, natural givenness. Only when redeeming faith does this, only when it sets man with all humility in the given orders and thereby in the midst of the world, so that what the redeemed man does there could also be done by any ordinary non-Christian who follows his rational insight into things, only then is redeeming faith really faith" (*Die Schuld der Kirche gegen die Welt* [Jena, 1930], pp. 44-45). In *Wider die Aechtung der Autorität*, he explicitly repudiated a contextualism that could give no definite direction to man's works (Jena, 1931, pp. 17-18).

speak of the final judgment which falls on the just and the unjust alike? Does the gospel give us no clues at all as to what *form* the historical orders discovered by reason should take? Is the Christian reduced to a kind of eschatological relativism which can only say that all men are sinners but can give no concrete direction to our works?

In order to answer these questions we should mention three factors—apart from the fundamental concern to preserve faith as pure faith—which have led Gogarten to speak on occasion as though faith and ethics stand in polarized indifference: 1) the desire to avoid the anarchy of a consistent contextualism, combined with 2) the equally strong desire to avoid moralism whether of the churchly-authoritarian or the liberal-optimistic type, and 3) most important of all, the conviction that the continued disintegration of the "orders" of society (family, state, etc.) will plunge Western culture ever deeper into chaos unless it can regain the fundamental binding force that comes only from the Christian faith. It is the tension between 2) and 3) which pushes Gogarten toward a paradoxical ethic, since he believes the binding power for Western culture cannot be found outside the Christian faith, yet refuses to derive this power from some form of Christian law. If it is faith which justifies and not works, then it is faith that will provide the binding force for civilization and not some kind of law. This basic insight, it seems to me, implies that faith must have an effect on *what* works are chosen, even though Gogarten's concern that faith not be turned into a kind of law, has meant he actually emphasizes the discontinuity of faith and ethics. The direction which faith gives to works is this: responsibility for the world is to be exercised in such a way that the structures and forms developed leave room for direct personal relationships. The criterion of ethical decision, therefore, is the understanding of human nature in terms of Christian personhood.

Unfortunately, this effort to find in Gogarten's concept of

personhood a more direct and concrete connection between faith and ethics cannot fully succeed since he conceives being and action in such a way that the active dimension of man's personhood could somehow operate in correlation with the receptive dimension, yet without the two really communicating in any *specific* way. It is no accident that Gogarten speaks of our action "leaving room" for personal relationships, since he seems to conceive the personhood of man as so exclusively interior that it cannot be touched by the structures of the world but somehow lives "between" them. Even when Gogarten says that the freedom for God is also freedom for the neighbor, the latter freedom has no tangibility or visibility. Gogarten can say, for example, that when a man is "liberated from the world and its determinations he does not stand before a void but before the neighbor. He stands before a neighbor who is not accessible in the predetermined relations of the world but only in the world-free openness of trust and love." [57] Here Gogarten in effect denies that faith gives any direction as to *what structures* will protect man's personhood but will only indicate how we should understand the *act of structuring as a whole*. Because being and act must be kept pure and undefiled from each other, Gogarten refuses to permit this general understanding of the limit of responsibility to have any direct influence on particular decisions. This seems to leave the man of faith living in two worlds which touch but never penetrate. Being and act are never really joined together in Gogarten's work but remain forever at the "bundling" stage. Of course it is only human to want to climb over the board, but this must never be permitted since it would violate the chaste receptivity of faith.

The same duality obviously besets Gogarten's understanding of the church with its radical distinction between the visible and

[57] VJC, p. 120.

invisible. Although the church is the immediate relation of persons to one another through the hearing and speaking of the Word, Gogarten offers no hint in his later works that this personal character of the community should affect its institutional structures. Moreover, since the task of the church is simply to keep the world secular by preserving man's awareness of the divine mystery in the world, it could not speak out on any specific social or political matters without betraying its own nature. It must be said that Gogarten derives what relevance the church has for ethics from the nature of the community of faith and not by ascribing to it a higher knowledge on ethical matters than the world has. His refusal to connect the being of the community with positive action by its institutional structures or even to grant some effect of the nature of the church on its institutional side fails to recognize that silence and conformity of the institutional church will be taken as assent to the *status quo.*

VI

GOGARTEN AND THE THEOLOGY OF SECULARIZATION TODAY

Bonhoeffer and Gogarten, although unlike in many ways, may nevertheless be linked as pioneers of the radical affirmation of secularization which has come to characterize much of current theology. Of course, the older liberal theologies also accepted secularization after their fashion, but they tried to mediate a place for religion in secular culture. The new radicalism derives its stringency from the sharp distinction between all "religion" and Christian faith. Secularization is not affirmed here out of any apologetic or mediating motives but because it is seen as the legitimate consequence of faith itself. Gogarten's particular contribution to this movement is his full-scale analysis

174

of the secularizing and historicizing implications of Christian faith and their radical application to all areas of theology. We can better measure the distinctiveness of his achievement, however, if we compare his position with several other contemporary efforts to come to grips with the problem of secularization.[1] For the sake of convenience, we may distinguish three basic types of approach to secularization which stand in contrast to Gogarten's affirmation of man's responsibility for a desacralized world. First, there are those who call for a recovery of the cosmic dimension of human life and therefore wish to turn secularization back in at least some respects. Secondly, there are those who hold that within limits secularization is consistent with Christian faith, but that the totality of secular experience must be transformed or sanctified. And finally, at the opposite extreme from the first view, are those who would not only deny any limit to the secularization of the world but would even accept a secularization of faith itself.

The perspective of the first tendency has been excellently stated by Walter J. Ong who laments modern man's incapacity to address God through an existential participation in nature and calls upon us to reunite the "interior and exterior, to restore man to his home in the cosmos." [2] It is Mircea Eliade, however, who has most impressively described urban man's impoverished religious sense. Even if the modern city dweller is a Christian, says Eliade, he "at most recognizes that he is responsible not only to God but also to history." But in these "man-God-history relationships there is no place for the cosmos." [3] This opposition between history and the sacrality of the cosmos is a persistent

---

[1] For a fuller discussion of various types of response to the problem of secularization, see my "Towards a Theology of Secularization," *Journal of Religion*, XLV (1965), 279-95.

[2] Walter J. Ong, "Religion, Scholarship, and the Restitution of Man," *Daedalus*. XCI (1962), 428-29.

[3] Mircea Eliade, *The Sacred and the Profane* (New York, 1961), pp. 178-79.

theme with Eliade. He argues, for example, that through the myths archaic man could participate in the paradigmatic models of primeval originative time (sacred) and thereby overcome the confusion and drift of mere evanescent duration or historicity (profane).[4] In general, those who regret man's loss of unity with the cosmos tend to see secularization as a process of desacralization that has so neutralized and devitalized nature and human life that man now lives almost totally in the profane, i.e., in mere history.

It would be unfair to suggest that those who call for a renewal of man's cosmic integrity are romantics who cannot stand the city and the machine, or are unaware of the difference between the Judeo-Christian understanding of faith in God and the sense of the sacred typical of the religions.[5] Nevertheless, in the light of Gogarten's case for the secularizing and historicizing power of Christian faith, any yearning to flee the radical historicity of existence would be both unchristian and illusory. It is unchristian because the historicizing of human existence is supported by faith itself, and it is illusory because you cannot return to a life of cosmic immediacy once its spell has been broken. After the divinities of the world have been neutralized and man has become self-knowingly responsible for agriculture, politics, and morality, there is no way back. In fact the very idea of a program to regain the integrity of man's sacral re-

[4] Ibid., pp. 17 and 68-72.

[5] Eliade suggests, however, that the desacralization of the cosmos has presented the theologian with a nonreligious man whose religious sense has dropped even beneath a "divided consciousness" by virtue of a "second fall" which has repressed it into the oblivion of the unconscious. The theological vocation would accordingly be a psychoanalytic one of bringing to consciousness this lost awareness of the sacred. But this assumes that Christian faith is fundamentally involved in the modality of the sacred. Eliade seems to hesitate between the secularizing implications of his admission that Judaism and Christianity evaluate linear history, and his view that this same acceptance of temporality actually sacralizes history by permitting the believer to participate in eternity here and now. (*Cosmos and History* [New York, 1959], p. 130.)

lation to the cosmos is a contradiction. How could we *produce* a natural relation to the world? The one great modern attempt to revive cosmic religion with its principle of religious-racial-political unity led to results that should give us pause. No doubt we are able to sense something of the structure of archaic man's life, but we will never be able to live it again without surrendering our independence and our technology. Of course archaic myths may one day elicit our response, but response is a historical and not an archaic phenomenon since it is always accompanied by a relationship of responsibility.

Yet Gogarten is far from disparaging the sacred, nor does he think that modern man's loss of a sense for the mystery of nature is an unalloyed benefit. In this respect it is important to remember that in Gogarten's concept of sin the being of the world is also inverted when man turns from the divine mystery. Correspondingly, the restoration of man to creaturehood is at the same time the restoration of the world to its being as creation. Creation is not a linear, causal relation between God and the world but God's "being with" man and the world.[6] For the Christian, the world, although not divine in itself, nevertheless remains unfathomable and alive because it is cared for by man as the inheritance intrusted to him. The turning of the inversion of being, therefore, could in one sense be spoken of as the redemption of nature. Nevertheless, the main thrust of Gogarten's understanding of creation remains historical rather than naturalistic since its principal elements are existential, e.g., man's encounter with his neighbor, his experience of nothingness when he tries to live on the basis of his own possibilities, his responsibility for the world before the divine mystery. Yet one is obviously led to ask if this does not make God the creator of man's existential life but not of the physical world. Although Gogarten has not given a direct answer to the question of the creation of nature, the basis for one kind of

[6] MZGW, p. 339.

answer is present in his idea that God's action as Creator is effective in the world through man's responsibility since man stands between God and the world. If we accepted a causalistic concept of creation, this would mean we might arrive at God on the basis of our knowledge of the world, and that sequence would deny the radical transcendence of God by putting the world between man and God. What if we were to start from the other direction, from the knowledge of God as the power which calls all things out of nothing into being? Would this not imply that the structure signified by God's "being with" the world and the actual state of affairs uncovered by natural science must at the least be mutually consonant? There would be two difficulties with attempting such a correspondence, however, 1) Gogarten's concept of God as absolute mystery is a limit concept which derives its content from our relation to this limit as it appears in the history of Jesus of Nazareth, and 2) the state of affairs uncovered by science is never that of the coherence of the world as a whole but is always limited by a particular field of reference. The only implication for natural science that could be drawn from God's presence with the world, therefore, is that science cannot answer the question of the coherence or wholeness of the world without ceasing to be science and becoming speculation. So long as science acknowledges the ultimately mysterious character of man and the universe and thereby refuses to spawn world views, its "godlessness" is the highest reverence for God.

The second approach to secularization which stands in contrast to Gogarten's position is represented by those who accept the secularity of political and economic institutions but insist that all facets of society must be premeated by the leaven of the sacred. Jacques Maritain, for example, speaks approvingly of a "secular Christian civilization" in which civil society will be autonomous in relation to the church and yet "recognize the quickening and inspiring role" that religious faith has to

178

play.[7] Thus secularization can be accepted as a normal process in the history of Christianity even though the Christian must constantly seek a "sanctification of the temporal order." [8] H. R. Niebuhr's transformationism leads to a more dialectical approach. He is convinced that radical monotheism means "a consistent secularization of all those symbolic objects that polytheism and henotheism meet with sacred fear and joy," and yet that the counterpart of this secularization is "the sanctification of all things." [9] Radical monotheism sweeps aside the traditional sacred/profane distinction and affirms the sacredness of *all* things, thus laying the "basis . . . not only of a transformed ethics, founded on the recognition that whatever is, is good, but of transformed piety or religion, founded on the realization that every being is holy." [10] Whereas Maritain calls for a transformation of the secular, Niebuhr sees the transcendent One transforming both the secular and the sacred. Everything is secular insofar as the sacred ceases to be localized, yet everything is sacred insofar as it is related to the One. All the transformationists have at least this in common, however: the secular is not to be left to its own devices but must be renewed or vivified by Christian faith.

Gogarten differs from the transformationists primarily in his emphasis on the necessity of keeping the world genuinely secular. He believes the danger we face in the modern world is not that economic and political life are being abandoned to their "own carnal law" (Maritain), but that they are always being infused with a holiness that does not belong to them. The task

[7] Maritain, *Range of Reason* (New York, 1952), p. 194.

[8] *Ibid.* Speaking of the historical succession of what he calls the sacral and the secular Christendom, Journet remarks that in the abstract the secular form of Christendom might have been the only one but for the historical circumstances of the Constantinian Empire. (Charles Journet, *The Church of the Word Incarnate* [London, 1955], pp. 220-21.)

[9] H. Richard Niebuhr, *Radical Monotheism and Western Culture* (New York, 1960), p. 52.

[10] *Ibid.*, p. 53.

of faith, as Gogarten sees it, is not to transform secularity but to keep man's responsibility limited to immanent and partial ends. Terror has not appeared where men have been concrete and pragmatic in their aims but precisely where they have re-sacralized political and social institutions. Gogarten argues that because Christian faith has radically reflected man back on himself and restored him to the responsibility of a son, he is empowered to take the risk of reason. Or as Carl Michalson so aptly put it, "Christianity tells us nothing we cannot find out for ourselves except that in Christ God has turned the world over to man." [11] Yet Gogarten does not regard the effect of faith on ethics as wholly negative. For the Christian's autonomy and responsibility is that of the son who perceives the mystery of his own being and being of the world and is therefore under no compulsion to give a final justification to his life through his works. Even for Gogarten the secular is transformed in the sense that the man of faith now sees the limits of the sphere of human autonomy as a whole.

So far we have placed Gogarten's theology against the background of positions more conservative than his own. Now we must turn to those who are ready to see faith itself secularized. In this country William Hamilton and Paul Van Buren are the best-known representatives of those prepared to jettison the sacred *in toto* and content themselves with an ethical perspective derived from Jesus. Van Buren comes to this position by virtue of a commitment to analytic philosophy which he sees as the embodiment of the inevitable empiricism of modern man. After defining secularism as the empiricist reaction against idealism, he finds his conceptual instruments for a secular theology in Hare's *blik* theory of religious language (Van Buren prefers to call *blik* a "historical perspective"). He replaces the

[11] Carl Michalson, *The Rationality of Faith* (New York, 1963), p. 155.

phrase "God the Father," which he believes analytic philosophy has shown to be either meaningless or misleading, with the assertion that faith consists of a single "orientation to the whole world." [12] Hamilton, on the other hand, begins with the more broadly conceived notion that, as a matter of cultural fact, God is *really* and not simply metaphorically dead, and that we must now move from the church "to the neighbor, to the city and to the world out of a sense of the loss of God." [13] Both are agreed that the disappearance of a reality which can be properly designated "God" still leaves room for a christological ethic. For Hamilton, faith is telescoped into love, a standing by others which is modeled on the historical Jesus.[14] Van Buren suggests that the disciples caught a new historical perspective at Easter which was a discernment situation in which Jesus was seen as "the man for others." [15]

By contrast, Gogarten's position on secularization obviously includes a "surd" that will not divide up without remainder into anyone's *blik.* Here is the real "inconsistency" of both Gogarten and Bultmann apart from which Gogarten believes theology becomes either pure philosophy or an exercise in intellectual history. From Van Buren's point of view, any talk about mystery or the question of wholeness, except in the sense of problems to be cleared up by linguistic sorting, is so much nonsense. From Gogarten's perspective, Van Buren's effort would represent a surrender before a subjectivism which insists that everything be determined by the subject in accord with pre-established principles of certification. Worst of all from Gogarten's point of view is the way both Hamilton and Van Buren turn Christian faith from pure justifying faith into an in-

[12] Paul Van Buren, *The Secular Meaning of the Gospel* (New York, 1962), p. 161.
[13] William Hamilton, "The Death of God Theology," *The Christian Scholar*, XLVIII (1965), 46.
[14] *Ibid.,* pp. 37, 46-47.
[15] Van Buren, *op. cit.,* pp. 132-34.

spiration and guide for moral action. To Gogarten this is simply to exchange the metaphysical misunderstanding of Christian faith for a moralistic misunderstanding. The issue between existential secularity *à la* Gogarten and empirical-ethical secularity *à la* Van Buren and Hamilton, therefore, is not whether the Christian man is autonomous and can live in a world ruled by technology and social planning, but whether the dimension of mystery or depth is essential to Christian faith. This is finally the question of the reality of faith, a question which for Van Buren at least must be answered in accord with the reigning (empiricist) notion of what is real. Of course, Gogarten himself is convinced that the problem of secularization can only be understood theologically through a discussion with the reigning idea of reality. But the discussion must not end in a simple capitulation to whatever seems most modern—not even to an existentialist position. For the discussion takes place because the thelogian stands between his world and the Word of God —not in order to meditate the two but to show the contemporary church where this Word comes into *collision* with our cultural presuppositions.

By delineating positions to either side of Gogarten, I have not meant to imply that he stands alone. On the contrary, his theological work as a whole obviously stands close to Bultmann, Ebeling, and Fuchs who take their cue from Gogarten (and Bonhoeffer) on secularization, and in America to Carl Michalson and Harvey Cox. Since *The Secular City* in particular exploits a number of Gogarten's basic motifs on secularization, it is perhaps worth pointing out some differences between Cox and Gogarten. The great virtue of Cox's discussion over Gogarten's rather intellectualistic approach is the way Cox strategically illuminates the theological analysis of secularization by linking it with the sociological study of urbanization. But offsetting the gain in concreteness and current relevance which Cox's sociological analysis brings to the problem is his tendency to idolize "technopolis" and the pragmatic man.[16] Closely connected with this celebration of urbanism is his misunderstanding of the I-Thou concept as a kind of ideal relationship which, since it cannot exist in the everyday encounters of city life, must be supplemented by an I-you concept to save these secondary relationships from being relegated to the evil of "I-it." [17] Gogarten's personalism (as well as Buber's), however, refers to the structure of reality defining man as man and not simply to an ideal relationship within that structure. If Cox had accepted the full import of this element in Gogarten's historical-personal approach to the theology of secularization, he might not have been drawn into portraying our current alternative as either a romantic rejection of technology and the city in favor of personalism, or the adultation of secular man's pragmatic formation of the polis as the sole form of Christian existence. Yet the deeper reason Gogarten does not feel compelled to absolutize either of these alternatives is that his understanding of the law is more complex than Cox's. Cox speaks of the law simply as a power from which we are freed by the gospel.[18] Gogarten understands the gospel not only as liberating us from the law but as sharpening or intensifying the law insofar as the gospel reveals that the heart of the law makes the same absolute demand which the gospel fulfills. Thus, if our particular historical-political location is the city, the gospel will meet us in the demands of our concrete responsibility for the shape of the metropolis (Winter). For Gogarten the good news

[16] This tendency is particularly apparent in Cox's critique of Tillich and Barth (pp. 78-84) and of Bultmann (pp. 252-53) which amounts to a sociologistic accusation of their theological inadequacy because they "breathe the air of the presecular *Bildungsschicht*" (p. 252). Here the shape and style of "technopolis" is erected into a theological criterion, but this same shape and style are not subjected to a theological critique—not even in the promising chapter suggestively entitled "The Church as Cultural Exorcist" (pp. 149-63).

[17] *Ibid.*, pp. 48-49.

[18] *Ibid.*, pp. 46-47, 208-12.

that we are given the freedom to fulfill our responsibility is also the overpowering destruction of our good conscience as happy pragmatists—for this gospel reveals that it is God himself who demands here, who demands more than could be expressed by any formulation of laws or norms. At the same time that the gospel buries us under this fantastic burden of responsibility, it says to us, "Nevertheless, you are free." For this gospel frees us from the bondage of an unfulfilled and—insofar as our *action* is concerned—unfulfillable responsibility. It declares us free to *be* responsible, since what we could not do has already been done. Another man like us has done for the world what we are called to do in the context of *our* historical situation. Therefore, we can give ourselves along with others of any faith or no faith at all to the task of planning and building the city and yet remain free of the alternate stridency and desperation which hounds every man who thinks he must fulfill the whole of this responsibility by human works. Gogarten would agree with Cox that God is to be met and spoken of "politically," i.e., in the concrete situation of the present.[19] But he would add as a corrective to Cox's work that, although the God of the gospel always meets us in the demands of our particular situation in the present (including the town or the jungle village), the single demand of the law which the gospel uncovers is never *identical* with the demands of the situation. If we fail to stress this difference, we cease to speak of revelation as history (or as politics) and instead speak of history or politics as revelation. Then we will have indeed fallen prey to an ideological form of secularism.

Now that we have seen Gogarten's work in the context of other efforts to meet the problem of secularization, we are in a better position to isolate his main contribution to the theological understanding of secularization. This contribution is twofold: first his insight that faith itself secularizes and historicizes

[19] *Ibid.,* pp. 249 ff.

the world, and second his understanding of this secularizing through the dialectic of law and gospel. These two factors in his analysis enable him both to affirm the total secularization of the world and yet combine this radical secularity with man's freedom for God. Gogarten conceives of the place of theological work to be between the Word of God and the world. Thus he comes to his solution to the problem of secularization on the one hand from an exegesis of the New Testament using Luther's rediscovery of man's freedom for God and for the world as his hermeneutic guide. On the other hand, he moves to his solution from his understanding of modern man's existence as fundamentally "historical," which is to say that the old metaphysical notion of two worlds—a merely passing world of time which depends on an eternal world beyond—is without meaning. Gogarten believes theology must respond to this demise of the natural-supernatural dualism by working out its concepts in terms of a single reality: history.

Historical reality has two dimensions both of which must be present if there is to be a genuinely historical existence for man and the world. To exist historically man must not only be responsible for what is to happen in the proximate future accessible to his planning but must carry out this anticipation by candidly exposing all that he has achieved and hopes to achieve to the menace of the future's impenetrable mystery. Most important of all, neither dimension can be telescoped into the other without aborting the constant genesis of historical existence. If a man were to try to secure himself against this incalculable imminence by his planning, he would stultify his capacity for change, whereas if he tried to assure his future by deriving an objectifiable "revelation" from its mystery, he would in effect destroy his responsibility and independence. In his book on secularization as a theological problem, Gogarten concisely expresses the twofold character of this history in a statement which may be taken as summarizing the basic intention of his theology of secularization:

All our deliberations are concerned with making clear that the highest and most proper business of faith is to husband the divine reality of salvation as it has occurred in the Cross and Resurrection of Jesus Christ, and at the same time to preserve and limit all human action to its earthly-worldly significance.[20]

This pattern of a single reality comprising two dimensions which must not be allowed to interfere with each other is the basic structure informing Gogarten's entire work, whether we look at the law-gospel motif, the duality of being and action, or the divine and human histories in the Christ event. It is at this point, accordingly, that critical discussion should be engaged. The crux of Gogarten's basic duality as a possible solution to the problems of secularization and subjectivism is whether the *unity* of the two dimensions is actually achieved. If these two dimensions are not *one* reality, we are merely left with a personalistic version of the natural-supernatural dualism. Gogarten conceives of this unity as a kind of relationship in which harmony is maintained by each side respecting the other's complete autonomy in its own sphere. The two are held together by faith. Thus faith, which is itself one side of the union over against works, is actually the dominant partner, responsible for maintaining the unity in distinction between itself and works. The difficulty with this solution, however, is that faith itself turns out to have two dimensions since it is both a mode of being which man receives and an act of decision. Gogarten seems to have repeated the very distinction he wishes to unite in the power which is supposed to maintain the unity. Of course the act of faith is a "deciding in being decided," and to that extent it permits man's history with God to be unified with his history with the world from moment to moment. Just as faith is not something decided once and for all, so the unity of the two dimensions must always take place anew. Thus the self-conscious act of the believer does not achieve the unity but only fights off the temptation to think the unity has happened or can happen merely through an act of man.

Even if we grant that Gogarten has accounted for a kind of unity between the divine and human histories or between being and act, it is a unity of a highly punctual sort. The main emphasis of his thought is on the necessity of keeping the two apart so that God may be God and the world may remain world (i.e., secular). Gogarten usually lets the two dimensions revolve around each other in suspension—as in his discussion of ethics. Or we are told, for example, that the active and receptive sides of man's being must never communicate even though there is a single person who lives "wholly out of works and wholly out of grace." But what sense can it make to speak of a "unity" when the very principle of unity seems to be that each dimension must remain totally insulated from direct and specific contact with the other? In the preceding chapters I have pointed out a few of the difficulties which result from this polarized indifference of being and act, interior and exterior: an unresolved problem of the priority of the hiddenness of God over his revelation, a partly unclarified relation between the historical reality of Jesus and the Jesus of the historian, an insufficient explanation of the *unity* of faith and works, and of the visible and invisible church.

These few comments on the conceptual framework of Gogarten's theology are merely a sketch of the kind of problems his work poses for us. His deepest concern since the beginning has been the question of the reality of faith; not the apologetic question, "Does faith have any reality by the prevailing standards of what is real?" but the aggressively theological question, "What is the reality proper to faith itself?" Of course this question is explored in *discussion* with the prevailing notion of reality. Yet it is not a concern to be "modern" which leads Gogarten to project theology as history but the conviction that the reality of faith is in fact historical in the special sense Gogarten gives to this term. As he remarked in an article on "Theology and History," he has no neat and simple answer to the question of theology and history but seeks to define somewhat more clearly what the question really involves.[21] He is quite aware that the understanding of historical reality he has been developing does not accord with some of the widely accepted uses of the word "history." But he is asking, what if the generally accepted view of what history is were mistaken? Suppose it is dominated by philosophical commitments which, by their currency in the modern period, have insinuated themselves into "common sense" discourse but are none the less historically conditioned? If this were in fact the case, would it not be strange for theology to treat this understanding of history, specifically the subject-object view, as indispensable to the reality of faith? Gogarten sees theology's task as the critique of the current conception of historical reality and historical knowledge as a necessary part of facing the acceptance of the historical-critical method in theology. Nevertheless, in the course of this critique theology must not try to develop a concept of history which can only be understood on the basis of faith since that would result in some form of "super-history" which is not genuine history at all; rather, the "understanding of history (*Geschichte*) which theology has cannot be one of which historical research (*Historie*) is incapable because the history which concerns revelation is of the same kind that concerns historical research." [22]

Gogarten is not suggesting that if we can only arrive at a

[21] ZThK, 1953, p. 341.
[22] *Ibid.*, p. 394.

subtler understanding of historical reality the major problems of pursuing theology in a secular context will all be solved. Obviously, it is equally incumbent upon us to do justice to the concept of nature—and even to that of supernature. After all, simply rejecting the cruder forms of supernaturalism or speculative metaphysics does not enfranchise us to ignore the better part of the Christian tradition and read only the New Testament and Luther. If our concern with historical reality leads directly to the question of the historicity of human existence, then we may even be able to learn something about historical reality from a "metaphysical" thinker who is concerned with the structure of reality which defines man as man even though he may have little to say explicitly on the subject of history. Moreover, in the British and American intellectual atmosphere our critique of the concept of history must be carried out in dialogue with the reigning empiricist tradition in its various forms. Some of Gogarten's particular formulations, therefore, will need to be "translated" for our situation since he not only presupposes the phenomenological critique of empiricism, but has also had to engage in a discussion with the idealist and existentialist currents which have dominated German thought in this century.

Gogarten has instructively explored many of the problems and possibilities which will be occupying us for a long time to come if we make a serious effort to wrestle with the secularization of history. Quite apart from his contribution to the more technical questions of theology, he has given us a theological interpretation of secularization which the church sorely needs precisely because of the current enthusiasm for a secular Christianity. If this new radicalism is not to dissipate into just another pose of avant-gardism, it must have a solid theological foundation. The gospel of secularization should be proclaimed only if it is Christian faith itself which brings the good news of man's freedom and responsibility for the world. A comprehensive theological demonstration that faith does in fact mean the liberation of man for the responsibility of a mature son is Gogarten's signal contribution to the Church's confrontation with a secularized world.

Appendix

BETWEEN THE TIMES
1914-1948

Gogarten has not always celebrated the maturity of man and the secularity of modern culture. In fact, his earlier work was pervaded by a contrary spirit, and it is only in 1948 that his "secular" theology begins to emerge. Although there are profound continuities in his thought, the importance of this shift toward secularization necessitates at least a brief outline of his theological development. His early theology, moreover, has an intrinsic interest because of the significant role he played in the rise and dissolution of the "dialectical school" of theology. Roughly speaking, there are five stages in Gogarten's work: 1) his early struggle for a viable understanding of religion within an idealistic framework, 2) his break with liberalism in the early 1920's, 3) the subsequent effort to supplant its idealistic basis with an interpersonal understanding of the nature of man and history, 4) his absorption with Germany's political crisis and the ensuing church struggle, 5) the postwar writings in which he reivses his earlier condemnation of modern "maturity" and turns to a positive appraisal of secularization.

1. *The Idealist*

It is significant for the direction of Gogarten's theological work that when he began his university training he was not headed for the pastorate or an academic career in theology but studied art history, German philology, and psychology. Although he admired a liberal pastor, Gottfried Taub, he felt he did not understand Christian preaching or the Bible. It was partly through the influence of Arthur Bonus' religiously oriented critique of secular culture and education that Gogarten decided to try theology. He studied first at Jena, then in Berlin under Harnack, and finally at Heidelberg where Troeltsch was still teaching on the theology faculty. But neither Harnack nor Troeltsch helped him to a satisfactory grasp of the meaning of Christian faith, and he turned to Tolstoy and German idealism in the hope of understanding what it was really about. Uncertain of whether to give up theology and turn to law or some other profession, he traveled to Switzerland where he came into contact with the work of Ragaz and Kutter. Then he spent several months in Florence enjoying the conversation of Arthur Bonus, playing the cello, and writing his first book, *Fichte as a Religious Thinker*.[1] It was only natural that in the first year of the War he should follow this book up with a pamphlet on *Religion and Nationality*. Here he not only

---

[1] Friedrich Gogarten, *Fichte als religiöser Denker* (Jena, 1914). I am indebted to Professor Gogarten for some of these early biographical details. There is also valuable material in the last chapter of Georg Merz's posthumous memoirs, *Wege und Wandlungen* (München, 1961), pp. 238-57.

asserted that the power of religion is drawn from nationality, but that war, far from being a punishment of God as the German bishops proclaimed, was a positive occasion for the rise of a new spirit in the people.[2] Gogarten had begun to read Luther and Kierkegaard as early as 1911, however, and they had been working on him. When his publisher Eugen Diederichs asked him to prepare a selection from Luther's works for 1917, Gogarten found himself unable to because, as Georg Merz reports him saying,

I read and read, but was stuck on the word "Jesus Christ." From everyone I had heard that it signified what the Idealists meant by "personality," the living "source in us," the "creative." Now I noticed this did not hold, that something else was meant by "Jesus Christ," an other, one who stands over against us.[3]

The book he did publish in 1917, *Religion from Afar,* shows Luther and Kierkegaard were beginning to have their effect, for its central thesis is that modern religious experience lacks the power of true individuality. Modern man knows only the individualism of having his own opinion and does not enter deeply into the experiences of guilt, thanksgiving, faith, love. But true individuality comes from afar—from the eternal. Although the concern with experience marks this little work as still largely within the liberal current, there is not only an echo of Kierkegaard but also a foreshadowing of the Thou-I and responsibility motifs which play such a large role in his

[2] Friedrich Gogarten, *Religion und Volkstum* (Jena, 1915). This pamphlet was put out by the neo-conservative magazine *Die Tat,* edited and published by Eugen Diederichs. In the light of the later political direction of Gogarten's thought, it is significant by comparison that Karl Barth's first great disillusionment with liberal theology was the fact that his former teachers in Germany signed a statement supporting the war policy of Wilhelm II. See "Evangelical Theology in the 19th Century," in Karl Barth, *The Humanity of God* (Richmond, 1960), p. 14.

[3] Merz, *op. cit.,* pp. 245-46.

critique of idealism. Gogarten writes of the modern understanding of fate:

He cannot free himself for experience, since that is finally possible only between an I and Thou. There must be two, who are both acting. In the modern experience of fate, there is only one actor. . . . Thus it is only a half-experience. That is seen also in the fact that what we call guilt is in effect excluded or repressed. . . . Yet guilt is nothing else than the expression for the responsibility that one takes upon himself in behalf of another.[4]

2. *The Break with Liberalism*

By the time *Religion from Afar* was published, Gogarten was pastor in a Thuringian village where he struggled with the responsibility of preaching to a people stunned and disillusioned by the war. Now he increasingly found his guide in Luther. It was during this same period that he briefly attached himself to the religious socialist movement. The Religious Socialist Congress held in Tambach in 1919—where he heard Karl Barth for the first time—and an invitation from Martin Rade to prepare a series of articles for the influential journal *Die Christliche Welt* forced him to take account of the distance he had traveled since 1914.

In the paragraphs he wrote for *Die Christliche Welt* under the title "Between the Times" he confessed that his generation could no longer listen to its liberal teachers whose world had gone crashing to the earth with the war.[5] The liberals, he said, taught us to look at all things as man's work, to see everything in its historical development. But now we use this medium to discover that man's work not only rises but also perishes, every-

[4] Friedrich Gogarten, *Religion weither* (Jena, 1917), pp. 14-15.
[5] Friedrich Gogarten, "Zwischen den Zeiten," *Die Christliche Welt*, 1920, p. 375.

where we see decomposition.[6] "We have all entered so deeply
into the human that we have lost God . . . there is no thought
in us any more that reaches Him." Yet even if we cannot think
God, "we know more certainly what He is not . . . we can no
longer deceive ourselves and mistake the human for the
divine." [7] The dream of salvation through cultural progress has
been dreamed out, and the stage is being cleared for the
question of God. Indeed "the times have fallen apart," but
we must not try to move from one time into another, *"we*
stand between the times." [8]

"Between the Times" made such an impression on its readers
that Gogarten was invited that year to address the annual
assembly of the "Friends of the Christian World" which
included most of the leading liberal theologians. The address
he gave stands along with Barth's *Epistle to the Romans* as a
turning point in contemporary theology: "The Crisis of Culture." Religion, said Gogarten, is always the crisis of culture,
a crisis from God. In this judgment of God on culture there
is no movement from man to God although there is always
the dialectic of God's "yes" along with his "no." Thus the
meaning of the postwar cultural and political crisis is the
judgment of God on the world.[9] The poet Wilhelm Schäfer
later described the effect of this address on the liberal audience:
"With Gogarten there stepped into the banqueting hall of the
Wartburg Martin Luther . . . ready to fling his ink bottle at
the head of the Devil. The man who there made his confession
was done with modern theology. The 'Friends of the Christian
World' had experienced the whip of God." [10] The address was

[6] *Ibid.,* p. 376.
[7] *Ibid.,* p. 377.
[8] *Ibid.,* p. 378.
[9] Friedrich Gogarten, *Die religiöse Entscheidung* (Jena, 1921), pp.
32-54.
[10] Quoted in John M'Connachie, "The Barthian School, III, Friedrich
Gogarten," *Expository Times,* 1931-32, p. 391.

printed in *Die Christliche Welt,* and overnight Gogarten became along with Barth a recognized spokesman of the theological revolt.

In the light of later developments it is important to notice that both these essays are not only a denial of theological liberalism but a rejection of the entire nineteenth-century liberal view of the world with its confident faith in rationalism, social organization, and humanitarianism. In short, they are a frontal attack on secularism. It is also interesting for what follows that Karl Barth did *not* reject political liberalism along with the liberal theology, but could say in his Tambach speech of 1919 that Christians must work within the socialist movement since "in democratic socialism *our* time meets the problem of opposition to the old order and is given the likeness of the Kingdom of God . . ." [11]

Originally acting in complete independence, Gogarten, Barth, and Brunner soon found themselves the leaders of a return to the Bible and the Reformers.[12] Characteristic of the spirit of amity in battle that marked those early days is Barth's letter to Eduard Thurneysen where he remarks that Gogarten's recent visit was "most delightful. There is a dreadnaught for us and against our opponents." [13] In 1922 the two pastors joined with Thurneysen and Georg Merz to found the theological journal *Zwischen den Zeiten* (*Between the Times*). For the next decade its pages were the meeting place of the new theological

[11] Karl Barth, *The Word of God and the Word of Man* (New York, 1938), p. 315. For a suggestive discussion of the interrelation of the political history of the 20's and 30's and the "Dialectical Theology" see Klaus Scholder, "Neuere deutsche Geschichte und Protestantische Theologie," *Evangelische Theologie,* 1963, pp. 510-36.

[12] Emil Brunner's break with liberal theology was first expressed in *Erlebnis, Erkenntnis und Glaube* (Zürich, 1921). In the Preface he calls attention to the second edition of Barth's *Römerbrief,* and to Gogarten's *Religiöse Entscheidung,* which had appeared shortly after he finished his own work (*ibid.,* p. iv).

[13] *Antwort, Karl Barth zum siebzigsten Geburtstag* (Zürich, 1956), p. 858.

tendency. Anyone who rereads the early issues cannot help being struck by the similarity in language of Barth, Gogarten, Brunner, Thurneysen, and Bultmann. Since one of the most familiar elements was the constant reference to the "no" and "yes," the judgment and mercy of God, the new theological direction was nicknamed "dialectical theology" or "theology of crisis." Yet neither of these titles appealed to them since their aim was, in Gogarten's words, "the only thing that can be the theme of an honest theology, to restore to the Word of God its rightful place in the execution of the theological task." [14]

Gogarten's initial attack on "liberalism" in 1920 and much of his subsequent work in the early twenties was centered on a critique of idealism and historicism, particularly as these were examplified in Ernst Troeltsch. Troeltsch's own comment on Gogarten's initial blast at culture-Protestantism was to charge his former student with setting up a sectarian either/or between religion and culture which showed that the young pastor had succumbed to the antihistoricism and irrationalism of the current generation; Gogarten, said Troeltsch, was a "romantic." [15] Gogarten retorted that Troeltsch was the romantic with his subjectivistic conflation of self, world, and God, and his concept of faith as a myth-forming "religious phantasy." [16] Gogarten's more considered criticism two years later, however, stressed his agreement with Troeltsch that theology cannot bypass the total historicizing of thought once it accepts the historical-critical method. His difference with Troeltsch falls at the point where Troeltsch's effort to overcome the relativistic implications of historicism ends in a flight from genuine history. The fundamental concept of Troeltsch's philosophy of history—

[14] Gogarten, *Gericht oder Skepsis*, p. 11.
[15] Ernst Troeltsch, "Ein Apfel vom Baume Kierkegaards," *Die Christliche Welt*, 1921, p. 189.
[16] Friedrich Gogarten, "Wider die romantische Theologie," *Die Christliche Welt*, 1922, p. 501.

individuality—points to the unique units or complexes which are the subject of historical study, wars, revolutions, the rise of capitalism, the development of Christianity, etc. Each individuality, according to Troeltsch, develops as the concretion of an ideal; it is a mixture of the relative and absolute, or, more specifically, it is "the essential and individual identity of the finite spirit with the infinite spirit." [17] This notion of the participation of the finite in the infinite, as Gogarten points out, is the basis of Troeltsch's solution to the problem of knowing other persons and other cultures (*das Fremdseelische*)—in contemporary terms, the problem of hermeneutics. The fundamental error of Troeltsch's position, according to Gogarten, is that Troeltsch reduces the actuality of historical occurrence to the individual's immediate participation in the infinite. Troeltsch's way of knowing the "other," for example, is not a genuine encounter with someone who is over against us, since the identity of the finite and infinite spirits means the "other" is already within the "I." Similarly Troeltsch's concern with the absolute and his search for the historically valid norms of Western culture do not touch the reality of God's encounter with man since the finite spirit participates directly in the infinite and its absolute values.[18] Thus the heart of the difficulty with both historicism and idealism is their individualistc understanding of man which results in an identification of the Word of God with human conscience. In the foreword to *Illusions, A Discussion with Culture-Idealism,* published in 1926, Gogarten said of this attempt to make culture a religious substitute:

Here we begin our opposition, because here is where modern man's "religion" begins: man's belief in himself, his belief in the soul and its "formation" of the world. Here the godlessness

---

[17] Friedrich Gogarten, "Historismus," *Zwischen den Zeiten,* 1924, p. 20.
[18] *Ibid.,* pp. 22-24.

of modern man is covered by a significant, pious garment: culture-formation, the attempt of modern man to create a religion with the help of a high-flying ethical ideology. In this religion man is God. That must be uncovered.[19]

3. *Theological Reconstruction*

Gogarten found the answer to liberal culture-Protestantism in Luther's understanding of the Word as the reality of man's life before God.[20] Along with Barth he also heartily endorsed Wilhelm Herrmann's contention that in the Word God gives himself and not simply information about himself. These two lines of thought led Gogarten directly to the development of his Thou-I motif. Although the Thou-I concept appears in Gogarten's writings as early as 1917, it was only in 1922 that he began to apply it systematically. In his collection of addresses *On Faith and Revelation* he acknowledges the influence of Ferdinand Ebner's *The Word and the Spiritual Realities* and of the discussions he had been carrying on with the Jena philosopher Eberhard Grisebach.[21] Since Gogarten developed his understanding of the Thou-I relation prior to the appearance of Buber's *I and Thou* (1923), it may be well to point out some of the differences between the two concepts. Buber's contrast is between personal and impersonal kinds of reality; I-Thou and I-it. Gogarten's contrast, however, is between I alone and Thou and I together, the contrast between solitude

[19] Gogarten, *Illusionen* (Jena, 1926), p. 2.

[20] Gogarten's view of Luther was in part worked out through a critical discussion with Karl Holl's research. Gogarten accepted much in Holl but objected to Holl's "Kantian" interpretation of Luther in terms of conscience. For Gogarten's review of Holl's major work on Luther, see *Die Christliche Welt*, 1924, pp. 34-42, 71-80, 121-22. Holl's reply later that same year is found on pages 307-14.

[21] Friedrich Gogarten, *Von Glauben und Offenbarung* (Jena, 1923), Preface and p. 79.

and community.[22] He uses the order *Thou*-I to stress the priority of the other person—in fact, he can even speak of the fundamental religious and ethical choice as Thou *or* I: the acceptance of the other as necessary to my being human, or the assertion of the I as the basis of reality. On this point the proximity to Grisebach is particularly marked.[23] What Gogarten wanted to convey through his Thou-I concept, therefore, was not a notion of affective spiritual communion, but the fact that what makes man human is his relation to others who are already there. Man is not first of all an individual who then establishes a relation to others, but first of all in relation so that the fundamental question is whether he will accept himself as existing through others or will live in contradiction to his true being. Gogarten came to this emphasis by way of his polemic against Troeltsch's identification of the I with the absolute which denies the otherness of God and the neighbor. Over against Troeltsch he had suggested in 1924 that the two constituent elements of history are the encounter with others and the encounter with God; the first gives history its content, the second prevents history from becoming a mere process and gives it the ambiguity which it must have if men are to be called to decision.[24] We have already traced Gogarten's development of this thesis in *I Believe in the Triune God* of 1926.[25]

But Gogarten soon found he was not only debating with the idealistic forms of German Protestantism but also with Karl Barth whose increasingly hostile jibes at Gogarten's efforts

[22] As Carl Michalson put it, for Gogarten "I without Thou is not history, for history is a community concept. I without Thou is reality in solitude; I with Thou is reality in love" (*Japanese Contributions to Christian Theology* [Philadelphia, 1960], p. 119). Buber comments on Gogarten's concept in *Die Schriften über das dialogische Prinzip* (Heidelberg, 1954), p. 296.

[23] See Eberhard Grisebach, *Die Grenzen des Erziehers und seine Verantwortung* (Halle, 1924).

[24] Gogarten, "Historicism," *Zwischen den Zeiten,* 1924, p. 22.

[25] See Chapter II, pp. 61-65.

to find an anthropological alternative to idealism gradually led to a parting of the ways. In fact the divergence between Barth and Gogarten began almost before the first issue of *Zwischen den Zeiten* was off the press, as we can see now from Barth's letters to Thurneysen in the early twenties. Particularly revealing is a letter of 1922 in which Barth complains that Gogarten was trying to do Christology "with the help of a speculative I-Thou philosophy. Heaven knows where that will yet lead. I am concerned for the future." [26] The gap between the two men did not become a complete break, however, until 1927 when Gogarten wrote a critical review of Barth's *Christian Dogmatics*. The basic defect Gogarten found in Barth's book was the lack of a clearly delineated anthropological anchor for its concepts. Gogarten agreed that theology must not derive its anthropology from a source outside theology. But because theological concepts are taken from the language of the world, each implies a definite understanding of man. Thus an adequate prolegomenon to dogmatics must clarify in what sense it uses these concepts by exposing the understanding of man and the world implicit in them.[27] Barth's reply was to charge Gogarten with returning to Schleiermacher and Ritschl, a charge he repeated and expanded in the first volume of the *Church Dogmatics* in 1932. The only clarification of concepts Barth would allow is one that takes place in the course of dogmatic research and not in the prolegomena.[28]

[26] *Gottesdienst-Menschendienst, Eduard Thurneysen zum 70. Geburtstag* (Zollikon, 1958), p. 47. With few exceptions the references to Gogarten in these letters are highly critical. Equally important, perhaps, is Barth's evident irritation at Gogarten's style and manner, especially his philosophical bent and his interest in getting a hearing among the "cultured despisers." Cf. pp. 27 and 44. But he could say of both Bultmann and Gogarten in a letter of 1925, "ten times better than Holl" (p. 134).

[27] Friedrich Gogarten, "Karl Barth's Dogmatik," *Theologische Rundschau,* 1929, pp. 66-67.

[28] Barth, *Church Dogmatics,* I, 1, 39 ff. and 141 ff. T. F. Torrance sees this clash with Gogarten as a key factor in pushing Barth toward his un-

The Secularization of History

As a result of his exchanges with Barth and of his new duties as *Privatdozent* at Jena beginning in 1925, Gogarten devoted several important addresses and essays to the question of theological method. In all of them he is battling two opponents: the reigning idealistic philosophy which turned theology into a rarefied species of intellectual history, and theological orthodoxy which sought refuge in traditional formulas and thereby deadened the impact of the living Word on contemporary history. Against the first tendency he asserted that theology must listen to the living Word spoken to it in the Scriptures and the preaching of the church.[29] Against orthodox archaism and Barth's refusal to join in the development of an anthropology appropriate for the needs of the time, he insisted that theology could only care for the living Word by "making clear the truth claim which this Word raises in our time, against our time, against our effort to withdraw from its truth. . . ."[30] Gogarten agreed with Barth that the error of Schleiermacher and the liberal tradition was to understand man first as a *homo religiosus* in order to move on to the *homo christianus*. But Gogarten saw the relation of anthropology and theology as circular:

One will never speak of man alone, but always at the same time of *that* God who has bound himself to this man in his revelation. On the other hand in theology one can never speak of God alone, but must always at the same time think of the man to whom he has made himself known in his revelation. It is evident that a circle is drawn by these two fundamental theses . . . there is no understanding of man without the understanding of God; but the reverse: the God . . . who has so indissolubly bound Himself to

compromising position on anthropology (Karl Barth, *An Introduction to His Early Theology* [London, 1962], p. 136).

[29] Friedrich Gogarten, *Theologische Tradition und theologische Arbeit* (Leipzig, 1927), pp. 4 and 20.

[30] Friedrich Gogarten, "Der Wahrheitsanspruch der Theologie," *Zeitschrift für Systematische Theologie,* 1931/1932, p. 479.

man that the being of this man is wholly dependent on God and directed to him—this God I cannot understand without already understanding man.[31]

Barth said he could accept this statement if only the word "already" were not in the last sentence, since "already understanding man" implied a theology based on a general conception of man.[32] But Gogarten believed we must "already" understand man since the truth in which the Christian believes is a historical one which can only be perceived historically. That means: to perceive the history of Jesus Christ as God's revelation is "first of all to know one's own history." [33] But in the encounter with the history of Jesus through the preaching of the church our own history is then known through his "being-for-us" as our "being-against" our neighbor. Therefore the actual relating of the "knowledge of Jesus Christ to the knowledge of ourselves is such that one is not prior to the other but only in and with the other." [34] It is important for understanding Gogarten's later view of secularization that he contrasts this historical truth of the believer who "belongs" to God and the neighbor through Christ with the attitude of what he here sarcastically refers to as the "mature" man of the modern period who considers himself the independent possessor of a timeless truth.[35] At this time (1931) Gogarten left the pastorate to become professor of systematic theology at Breslau. In 1935 he was called to Göttingen where he has remained since, becoming professor *emeritus* in 1955.

[31] Friedrich Gogarten, "Das Problem einer theologischen Anthropologie," *Zwischen den Zeiten,* 1929, p. 496.

[32] Barth, *Church Dogmatics,* I, 1, 145.

[33] Friedrich Gogarten, "Wahrheit und Gewissheit," *Zwischen den Zeiten,* 1930, p. 108.

[34] *Ibid.,* p. 111.

[35] *Ibid.,* pp. 107 and 113.

4. *Theology and Politics*

The fateful tendency in Gogarten's thought of the period after 1926 was the way in which he applied the Thou-I anthropology he was developing to the political questions of the day. He saw the source of the dissolution of the fundamental orders of society in the spiritual ethos of the intellectual bourgeoisie for whom the highest value is the autonomous I, the free personality. The Thou-I concept not only helped Gogarten appropriate the Lutheran doctrine of the orders but also offered a way of justifying the need for authority in political life. In all his writings of this period he incessantly battles the idea that individual freedom is the essence of Protestantism, arguing instead that obligation (*Hörigkeit*) is the key to the Reformation's understanding of man. By obligation he did not mean an external, legalistic bondage to throne or altar but the concrete existential bond with God and the neighbor. The task of Protestantism, he argued, is to give the world the knowledge of this bond since only in a real belonging to one another do we have true freedom, the freedom from ourselves.[36] This belonging is not a matter of two individuals coming together in an indeterminate I-Thou relation, but the concrete bond with each other through our positions in life whether it be as parent, employer, worker, or any other capacity. Thus Gogarten's interpersonal understanding of human nature enabled him to avoid the rigidity of an abstract scheme of "creation orders" while nevertheless recognizing the total political order as ordained by God. Just as there is only faith in

[36] Gogarten, *Glaube und Wirklichkeit*, pp. 18 ff. Although in this work Gogarten uses *Bindung* rather than *Hörigkeit*, the latter comes to dominate his ethical discussions. Its literal meaning is "bondage" but Gogarten uses it to express his conviction that men "belong" (*gehören*) to each other by "listening" (*hören*) to the word of the other. *Hörigkeit* stands for Gogarten's concept of man as "being-from-the-other" and "being-for-the-other." Cf. *Politische Ethik*, pp. 20, 32 ff.

God in the concrete relationships with my neighbor, so there is no eternally valid knowledge of the orders of creation in general but only "the concrete listening to the claim of the other and, in this receptivity, the concrete knowledge of one's own responsibility." [37] Although he recognized the concreteness and historicity of the orders, Gogarten rejected the eschatological relativism of those who said in effect that so long as we do not bow the knee to Baal, it makes little difference what cultural or political views we take. [38] On the contrary, Gogarten argued, even if the church cannot prescribe certain forms of government, it can help the world see that some alternatives, such as anarchy, are excluded. Moreover, it can refute the spurious individualism of the modern spirit with its neurotic fear of all authority, and it can point to the fact of actual inequalities among men and man's inevitable violation of the fundamental bond of his life which necessitates authority backed up by force in order to keep men from devouring one another. [39] The issue today is no longer what form authority and force should take, but whether there should be any authority in political life at all. [40]

Gogarten's concern with a theological understanding of the political situation of the Weimar Republic came to a head in his *Political Ethics* of 1932. This complex and disturbing book not only contains magnificent passages on man's being-from-others and being-for-others, but also a somber endorsement of the grandeur of the state as the instrument of God to restrain evil. The *Political Ethics* deepens Gogarten's analysis of the foundation of ethics and underlines his thesis that the

[37] Gogarten, *Ich glaube an den dreieinigen Gott*, p. 211.

[38] Even T. F. Torrance admits that Barth's theology in the late twenties was unable to get beyond a paradoxical relation of theology and culture (*op. cit.*, pp. 138-39).

[39] Gogarten, *Wider die Aechtung der Autorität* (Jena, 1930), pp. 21-23.

[40] *Ibid.*, p. 44.

necessity of political order should be understood from the fact of man's actual alienation from his fellows. The fundamental ethical phenomenon can be discerned in the "Thou shalt" sense of an ethical demand as contrasted with the "one does it" sense. When we say "one should not steal," we imply an "if" clause which indicates the deed is to be avoided in order to remain acceptable to those who hold the same set of values. The "Thou shalt" sense of the demand, however, calls a man out of the accepted values and moral conventions and shows him the impossibility of fulfilling the total demand implied in "Thou shalt!" The "one does it" sense of an imperative says "avoid killing," but the "Thou shalt" sense says "you are already a murderer at heart." [41] Thus the fundamental ethical phenomenon exposed by the "Thou shalt" is that man, who is created with others and for others, lives in contradiction to his true nature. Man is seen as evil. By "evil" Gogarten did not mean that man is a cauldron of hate and vile desire; the evil here is more fundamental than passions—it is the inversion of the structure of man's being-with-others.[42]

The one who hears the "Thou shalt" does in fact resist his being-from-the-other. He exists as a self in the mode of contradiction. It is a contradiction against the truth of himself. In so far as he listens to the "Thou shalt" he stands between the truth of himself and the lie of himself . . . between his being-from-the-other and his being-against-the-other.[43]

[41] Gogarten, *Politische Ethik,* pp. 8-12. Gogarten elaborates on the two senses of the ethical command by showing the two concepts of the self which are implied in each.

[42] *Ibid.,* pp. 50-51.

[43] *Ibid.,* p. 34. Brunner uses this concept in his anthropology, *Man in Revolt* (London, 1939), whose literally translated title is "Man in Contradiction" (*Der Mensch im Widerspruch* [Berlin, 1937]). There is a great similarity between Gogarten's early work and Brunner's *Man in Revolt* and *Truth as Encounter* (Philadelphia, 1964; *Wahrheit als Begegnung,* Berlin, 1938). The most essential element in common is their understanding of man's

The state exists to preserve man's external being from others by enforcing the respect due the "positions." [44] When it ensures that men honor their obligations to one another, the state protects and enforces all the other orders and makes a genuinely human life possible.[45] Gogarten could even say of the state or *politia*, which erects these barriers to man's refusal of his fellowmen, that "there is no greater gift of God on earth because it is the most comprehensive and fundamental of the orders of human life." [46]

In the *Political Ethics* Gogarten claims that the purpose of his writings on politics at this time is simply to show the contemporary relevance of Luther's statement that God wants man to serve him in his "position" and not in self-chosen works.[47] Insofar as the Christian works within the political structures, his works are "good" and pleasing to God even though the one who does them is not good. Correspondingly the task of the church cannot be moral guidance but the strict preaching of the gospel which holds before man the "Thou shalt" sense of the ethical demand and reveals his need of the polis.[48] By this preaching the state is kept aware of the radical evil of man and of its own limited purpose of preserving the external existence of man. For the danger of the state is that it always tends to go beyond the preservation of human life and tries to become the foundation of man's whole existence. In 1932, Gogarten saw this danger threatening the German state in the nationalistic movement which wanted to make

---

original life as being-in-response. Brunner's basic thesis is that "even the unbeliever is still related to God, and therefore that he is responsible, and that this responsibility is not put out of action even by the fullest emphasis upon the generous grace of God, but, on the contrary, that God requires it" (*Man in Revolt*, p. 11).

[44] Gogarten, *Politische Ethik*, pp. 198-202.
[45] *Ibid.*, p. 109.
[46] *Ibid.*, p. 113.
[47] *Ibid.*, p. 166.
[48] *Ibid.*, pp. 218-20.

the state an instrument of the nation. He warned that to seek the foundation of the state in the nation rather than in the gospel—which reveals the alienation of men that makes the state necessary, is to turn the nation into a substitute for God.[49]

By the summer of 1933, Hitler was gathering the full reins of the state into his hands and even reaching out for the Evangelical Church by siding with the "German Christians" in the church election of July, 1933. The German Christians wanted to enlist the church's support for the new regime and carry out such "reforms" as the creation of a Reich's bishop in conformity with the "Führer" principle. Gogarten briefly sided with the German Christians that summer and made it clear he regarded the demise of the "individualistic" and "anarchistic" Weimar Republic as a positive opportunity for the church. Most compromising of all from our contemporary point of view was his polemic against the chief opposition to the German Christians: the Confessing Church and its theological leader, Barth. Certainly Gogarten was never a National Socialist, and he rejected the infamous German Christians only a few months after the church elections when it became clear they wanted to eliminate the Old Testament and exclude from the church persons of Jewish blood.[50] And in 1936 he signed a statement along with Bultmann, Althaus, and several others refuting the German Christian position.

[49] *Ibid.*, pp. 212-13. For Buber's reaction to the *Politische Ethik,* see *Between Man and Man* (London, 1947), pp. 76-79.

[50] Gogarten made his rejection of the "German Christians" known the day after the infamous address of Krause in the Berlin *Sportpalast* on November 13, 1933. Cf. Theodor Strohm, *Konservative politische Romantik in den theologischen Frühschriften Friedrich Gogartens* (Berlin, 1961), pp. 190-91. Although there are a number of helpful observations in Strom's thesis, he has distorted the character of Gogarten's theological understanding by starting with a definition of "political romanticism" taken from Tillich, which he proceeds to "apply" to Gogarten's work in a systematic fashion. For the background and ideology of the "German Christians" see Hans Buchheim, *Glaubenskrise im Dritten Reich* (Stuttgart, 1953).

Nevertheless one cannot help asking how Gogarten, who had once spoken of religion as the crisis of culture and had only the year before warned against nationalism, could have regarded National Socialism as anything but a deadly temptation. Naturally we cannot fully answer this question within the scope of our present survey, but some effort must be made if we are to understand why a theologian of Gogarten's stature could make the choice he did.[51] This question also turns out to be significant for the problem of secularization since one of the major factors in his decision was the conviction that secularization (=autonomy) and Christian faith are mutually exclusive, and this quite naturally drew him toward the conservative political thinkers who helped prepare the downfall of the Weimar Republic.

One of the most important clues to Gogarten's political position, therefore, is that his break with liberal theology was a rejection of political and cultural liberalism. Gogarten himself called attention to this in 1937 when he wrote that the general crisis following the First World War was not without influence on the radicalism of him and Barth, and that it was the difference in the way they understood this crisis which marked the deep opposition that was present from the beginning even in what they held in common.[52] In the introduction to *Political Ethics* he speaks of the War as the end of the epoch of humanism, the end of the dream that man is lord of himself and the

[51] Franklin Littell, who has done as much as anyone in America to foster the study of the Church Struggle, has said of the standard oversimplified picture of this time, "a certain amount of 'de-mythologizing' of the Church Struggle will be necessary before the true view begins to emerge" ("Current Study of the Church Struggle with Nazism and its significance for Church History," a paper read April 8, 1960, at the American Society of Church History and circulated in mimeographed form as part of Newsletter #4 of the American Committee on the History of the Church Struggle with Nazism, F. H. Littell, ed., August 1, 1960, 2). See also John S. Conway, "The Historiography of the German Church Struggle," *The Journal of Bible and Religion*, 1964, pp. 221-30.

[52] Gogarten, *Gericht oder Skepsis?* p. 13.

The Secularization of History

world.[53] In another work of the same year he speaks of the "unbounded dominion of man over the world" as the great presupposition of the modern period. This dominion means both the desacralization of the world and an unlimited faith in man.[54]

Gogarten's rejection of the humanist and Enlightenment ethos was hardly original. Liberalism (the "West") had been under attack by a large segment of the German intelligentsia throughout the nineteenth century—one need mention only Schopenhauer and Nietzsche or the more popularly influential Julius Langbehn and Paul de Lagarde. After the War the anti-liberal, anti-Western tendency found many representatives ranging from Thomas Mann and Ernst Jünger to Oswald Spengler and Moeller van den Bruck.[55] Although Gogarten was critical of some aspects of their "conservative revolution" tendencies, he shared their rejection of the secularism and liberalism of the West and saw the only hope for a genuine political life in turning away from Western individualism and revitalizing the life of the German people. Gogarten also shared a number of positive concerns with the conservatives—an emphasis on decision in the presence of the demand of one's historical destiny,[56] a definition of freedom in terms of the libera-

[53] Gogarten, *Politische Ethik,* p. 1. An important essay of 1937, in fact, is entitled *The Collapse of Humanism and the Question of God.*

[54] Friedrich Gogarten, *Weltanschauung und Glaube* (Jena, 1937), p. 39 (first published in 1932 as *Die Selbstverständlichkeiten unserer Zeit und der Glaube*).

[55] There is a growing body of literature on the background of the "neo-conservative" movement. Among the most helpful works in English are Fritz Stern's *The Politics of Cultural Despair* (Berkeley, 1961), and Klemens von Klemperer, *Germany's New Conservativism* (Princeton, 1957). In German the pioneering study is Armin Mohler's *Die Konservative Revolution in Deutschland* (Stuttgart, 1950). The best recent survey is Kurt Sontheimer's *Antidemokratisches Denken in der Weimarer Republik* (München, 1962).

[56] On this aspect of neo-conservativism, see Karl Löwith's essay, "Der okkasionelle Dezisionismus von C. Schmitt," in Karl Löwith, *Gesammelte Abhandlungen* (Stuttgart, 1960), pp. 93-126; and Christian Graf von

210

tion experienced in accepting the obligation to the state and nation,[57] the conviction that the true state has its authority and power in itself and not from a social contract,[58] and finally the belief in the *Volk* as the basis of human community and the ultimate source of ethical norms.[59]

An understanding of the *"Volk"* concept in particular is important not only for grasping the political and religious debate of the time but also for seeing its relevance to the problem of secularization. Broad enough to carry the connotations of both nationality and race, the *Volk* concept also points to the social and moral customs of the common people, who supposedly produce "folk" music and "folk" tales. In the tradition behind the conservative revolution tendency, the *Volk* was regarded as a sort of mystic entity, an organic unity of pure racial stock typified by the unspoiled peasant.[60] Gogarten agreed with the conservatives that the orders of life such as the *Volk* are not the product of man's rational control of life; man can only form and care for orders that are already there.[61] But Gogarten denied the prevalent idea that the *Volk* is an organism to be identified with blood or race.[62] Instead he interpreted it in terms of the Thou-I motif as an expression of the creational bond between man and man. The concrete manifestation of this bond is the living morality of the *Volk* in which man experiences a real law that binds him to others rather than the sham law of individualism which can only bring chaos.

Krockow, *Die Entscheidung, eine Untersuchung über E. Jünger, C. Schmitt, M. Heidegger* (Stuttgart, 1958). One should be careful not simply to identify one concept of decision with another, as Löwith tends to do in equating Gogarten's use of the term in "Entscheidung im Nichts" with the concepts of Heidegger and Schmitt (*op. cit.*, pp. 214-26).

[57] Sontheimer, *op. cit.*, pp. 337 ff.
[58] *Ibid.*, pp. 240 ff.
[59] *Ibid.*, pp. 308 ff.
[60] Stern, *op. cit.*, pp. 368, 87, 139 ff.
[61] Gogarten, *Das Bekenntnis der Kirche*, p. 9.
[62] Friedrich Gogarten, "Schöpfung und Volkstum," *Zwischen den Zeiten,* 1932, p. 501.

Today, Gogarten warned, even the *Volk* is treated in the manner of Western individualism with some seeking their salvation in a religiosity that has race and nationality as its idols. Only in believing in Jesus Christ can we recognize our nationality as the gift of God the Creator.[63]

If we put Gogarten's antiliberalism and antisecularism together with his concept of the state and his understanding of the *Volk*, we have the political-cultural background of his decision in 1933. The theological debate in which he played a major role revolved around the question of law and gospel (or revelation and history). The "German Christians" had pushed this issue to the center by asserting that "the law of the *Volk* is the law of God." Gogarten qualified their slogan to read "the law of God is met *in* the law of the *Volk*," basing his view on the traditional distinction between the theological and the political use of the law. The former is the primordial and essential form of the law, the naked command of the Creator, which reduces man's pretension to ashes and "drives him to Christ." The latter use is the derivative and particularized form of the law, the individual commands which man is able to fulfill and thereby preserve the order necessary for human life.[64] The pivotal issue for Gogarten was his claim that these particular commands of the "political" use are not to be found in the Bible or in an ethic derived from the Bible but are experienced in the concrete historical orders of life, above all in "the morality of the *Volk* and the law of the state." [65] However, the relation of the two forms of the law is not such that the present demands of these orders are unambiguously and directly the law of God; rather they are his

[63] *Ibid.*, pp. 503-4. Although Gogarten himself condemned racism, he was willing to see in the "respect" for racial purity a reflection of pious reverence for the God-given orders of life (*Das Bekenntnis der Kirche*, pp. 44-45).
[64] Friedrich Gogarten, "Volkstum und Gottesgesetz," *Deutsche Theologie*, 1934, pp. 83-85.
[65] Gogarten, *Das Bekenntnis der Kirche*, p. 31.

law only in the sense that he never meets man apart from the specific obligations of historical life. Hidden in all the orders or boundaries of everyday life lies the single fundamental boundary—that man owes his life to God and the neighbor, and this demand may break out from the midst of any particular relationship or situation.[66] Since Gogarten did not conceive of the orders of creation as static but as developing through the "risk of reason," he could view a historical event which radically altered the political order as the place where —at that moment—the law of God was to be encountered in its *usus politicus*.[67] And we can see how this would be especially true if the particular event were one that cleared away the remnants of the bourgeois individualism which Gogarten believed to be irreconcilable with the authority and power of a genuine state.[68] For under the "pseudo-state" of the Weimar Republic, based as it was on the idea of the absolute autonomy of the individual, men could hardly experience the law at all and consequently they could not really know the liberating power of the gospel.[69] In 1937, looking back at his decision of 1933, he wrote:

When I announced my support of the "German Christians" it was strictly because this decisive thesis [the law is given in our national life] preserved the openness of the Church to the world and its historical life, and because I saw the ecclesiastical opposition driving the Church into an "independence" which would harden it in the spiritual habitus of nineteenth-century bourgeois individualism (whether with or without a repristinated orthodoxy), and shut it up in itself and isolate it from the historical life of our

[66] *Ibid.*, p. 39.
[67] For this application of the Law-Gospel theme see "Offenbarung und Geschichte," *Deutsche Theologie*, 1935, pp. 115-31. The "risk of reason" concept is developed in *Das Bekenntnis der Kirche*, pp. 27 ff.
[68] Friedrich Gogarten, "Staat und Kirche," *Zwischen den Zeiten*, 1932, pp. 402-5.
[69] Gogarten, *Ist Volksgesetz Gottesgesetz?* p. 30.

people. This danger seemed greater to me than those which threatened from the "German Christian" side, and for which I have certainly not been blind.[70]

As a result of Gogarten's stand Barth wrote his famous "Parting" to *Zwischen den Zeiten* in which he accused Gogarten of identifying the law of God with the historical demands of the *Volk*. This was a direction, said Barth, toward which Gogarten had been heading all along, moving from an "investigation of the genuine concept of history by way of the doctrine of Thou and I to the ever more massive dogma of the orders." [71] With such a man, Barth said, he could no longer be associated; even the founding of *Zwischen den Zeiten* had been a misunderstanding.[72] In the same issue with Barth's essay, Merz printed a letter from Gogarten which expressed regret over Barth's decision to withdraw and set forth his own understanding of the kind of theological discussion needed just then.

You are quite aware that I am convinced that we who have learned our theology from the Reformers have today not only a negative, protesting task but a positive one too. However confused their claims may be, one must speak differently to the claims of the state and *Volk* than to the unreal claims of culture-Protestantism. . . . One must have taken earnestly state and *Volk* which (I will express myself cautiously) have to do with Law and in some way deal with or represent Law, in order to be able to turn against them in the name of the Gospel when they over-step their boundaries.[73]

Although Gogarten sided with those Lutherans who were willing to work out some kind of *modus vivendi* with the state,

---

[70] Gogarten, *Gericht oder Skepsis?* pp. 8-9.
[71] Karl Barth, "Abschied," *Zwischen den Zeiten*, 1933, pp. 538-39.
[72] *Ibid.*, p. 541.
[73] Quoted by Merz in *Zwischen den Zeiten*, 1933, p. 552.

by 1936 he himself saw that the point of theological dissent had in fact been reached and signed a statement condemning the main theses of the "German Christians." The second paragraph of this "opinion" criticizes the "German-Christian" identification of the church with the *Volk*. The church has a particular historical form in each nation, "but as the church of Christ it always stands distinct and independent of all nationalities." [74] The paragraph which follows is directed at the political commitment of the "German Christians."

The false identification of nation and Church corresponds to the *false identification of national history and salvation history*. The knowledge that God deals with the German people in their history as he does with all other nations is falsified in a philosophy of history that makes . . . the Germans the saving people for the whole world.[75]

The fourth paragraph condemns the "German Christian" view that the Christian faith is a belief in the "task of the historical situation as a divine demand." On the contrary, the sole object of Christian belief is "God's revelation in Jesus Christ." [76] It is sadly ironic that the condemnation of the "German Christians" that Gogarten helped write in 1936 is remarkably close to the protest of the Confessing Church at Barmen in 1934.

As a result of the church struggle both Barth and Gogarten were forced to spell out more fully their positions on law and gospel (or gospel and law, as in Barth). In the early debate Barth's primary criticism had been that a view of law and

---

[74] Heinrich Hermelink, *Kirche im Kampf. Dokumente des Widerstandes und des Aufbaus in der evangelischen Kirche Deutschlands von 1933 bis 1945.* (Tübingen and Stuttgart, 1950), p. 339.

[75] *Ibid.*

[76] *Ibid.*, p. 340.

gospel like Gogarten's must of necessity lead him to make events of world history a second source of revelation. Gogarten retorted that Barth's dualism of "Scripture or 1933" was an impossible one since Barth listened to the events of 1933 just as much as he did, only each of them heard different things.[77] In 1937 Gogarten climaxed his reply with a polemical book which charged that Barth's position was based on an abstract dialetic of time and eternity which led to a generalized skepticism about culture rather than to a genuine witness of divine judgment.[78] In retrospect it is easy to see that at the time it was Barth's criticism of Gogarten which hit the mark, since Gogarten spoke as though the church could not really preach the gospel to secularized men, but had to presuppose a man living under the religious power of the *Volk*. The tragedy of Gogarten's position in the church struggle was his misjudgment of both the National Socialists and the Confessing Church. He was deceived by the antiliberalism and antisecularism of the former and offended by the conservative ecclesiasticism of the latter. In particular his obsession with the problem of individualism did not allow him to see the ethos of the conservative revolution tendency as itself one of the self-evident truths *against* which the church must confess the Word of God. Nevertheless we cannot attribute his decision purely to a misreading of the situation but must leave standing the question which the church struggle unavoidably puts to anyone who wants to follow Gogarten on law and gospel.

5. *Theological Reappraisal*

In 1938 Gogarten suffered a serious illness which prevented him from productive work for a considerable time. His thought

[77] Gogarten, *Das Bekenntnis der Kirche*, p. 25.
[78] Gogarten, *Gericht oder Skepsis? Eine Streitschrift gegen Karl Barth*, esp. pp. 150 and 155.

in this period, as evidenced by two books which appeared in 1948, had been turned to a reappraisal of his understanding of the secular ethos of Western liberalism which had been so fateful for his work in the thirties. It is striking that both he and Bonhoeffer should at the same time and independently of each other come to the conclusion that the ideal of autonomy and freedom is not in itself the enemy of Christian faith but an approximation of the worldliness and responsibility of faith itself. There seems little reason to doubt that it was the degeneration of the "renewal" of state and *Volk* into a racist and expansionist fanaticism that stimulated his new appreciation of the Western liberal tradition. In *The Preaching of Jesus Christ* published in 1948 he wrote that although the catastrophe which had occurred could be traced in the "inconceivable but nevertheless successful rise of an inhuman cruelty and in the unbounded indifference to the most self-evident human rights," even more frightening than the actual brutalities is the "sheer unresisting capacity for them which has taken hold of contemporary men of all social classes and educational levels." [79] He went on to suggest that this collapse of humanity cannot be fully understood in political or legal or even moral terms, but points to a deeper source. The trials of war criminals, he said, do not touch the profounder question of German guilt, since "the fact that a man did not take an active part in the excesses is no proof that this decay of fundamental humanity has not touched him." [80] The root of the problem, as Gogarten sees it here, is that man, having lost God as his counterpart has also ceased to understand that he only has life through his fellowmen.[81] Thus Gogarten's analysis of German guilt is theologically of a piece with his prewar personalism, especially that of *I Believe in the Triune God*. Yet he now gives equal

[79] VJC, p. 490.
[80] *Ibid.*, pp. 488 and 490.
[81] *Ibid.*, pp. 486-87.

weight to the "independence" or autonomy of man and no longer equates being-from-the-other with belonging to state and *Volk*. This shift is particularly explicit in another work of 1948, *The Church in the World,* which interprets National Socialism in the context of the problem of secularization. Here Gogarten sees the German experiment of the 1930's as an attempt to make the *Volk* the all-embracing structure from which man was to derive his total existence. The reason the effort had to prove abortive was that secularization has created a situation of human responsibility for history. And once man has taken on responsibility for the world, he cannot return to a "natural" life in which he is immediately united with the *Volk*.[82] According to Gogarten, this is why nationalism which long ago replaced Christianity as the spiritual force of the Western world, always has an internal drive of self-aggrandizement. The nation can no longer be a natural reality; it is an ideal to be achieved. This is the root of the modern bent for totalitarianism which destroys the freedom of man by manipulating people in behalf of a social ideal. In building the ideal society the modern state knows no limits so long as those who are leading it consider man himself the ultimate power in the universe.[83] Gogarten sees the postwar struggle against nationalism in the name of the rights of man as the struggle to keep the state and society secular and not let it become a totalitarian power. In this battle the church must be on the side of secularization.[84]

Whereas he once joined the "conservative revolution" in condemning secularization and liberalism, Gogarten now views the attack on individualism in the name of the *Volk* as an attempt to return to a pre-Christian unity of politics and religion. He has reversed his estimate of the Enlightenment

[82] KW, p. 11.
[83] *Ibid.,* p. 12.
[84] *Ibid.,* pp. 21-22, 25-26.

slogans of autonomy, freedom, and independence to the point that he now regards them as essential expressions of one dimension of Christian faith. Nevertheless, he has retained those elements of his critique of individualism which grew out of the Thou-I concept. For he is still convinced that if man considers his autonomy and freedom to be the product of his own will and does not acknowledge their ground in his relation to God and the neighbor, there will be no limit to what he may do to himself and to others.

It would seem to follow from this that not only the "right" but also the necessity of rebellion are established. But whereas Gogarten's break with his political position in the 1930's has led him to affirm man's responsibility for the world, he has not taken up the question of political ethics in the context of his new understanding of secularization. One cannot help wondering if his almost exclusive emphasis on preserving the secularity of the world is a sufficient corrective of his previous position. For if we are to learn anything from the situation of the German church in 1933, it is that the Christian cannot simply wait to see if a political change will result in the state's stepping beyond its secular responsibilities and claiming to be the basis of man's life as a whole. By the time the state has gone that far it will be to late to do anything about it. The source of this difficulty would seem to lie in Gogarten's understanding of the law. For having accepted from Troeltsch the idea of the historical relativity of all norms, Gogarten has resolutely turned away from either a revealed biblical ethic or a traditional natural law ethic. His answer to relativism and individualism, therefore, could only be to sanction the developing institutions and norms of society as expressions of the "political" use of the law. But even though these historical forms are not *identical* with the law of God in Gogarten's thought, there is no way to criticize any particular political institution or political action on the basis of divine law. When in his postwar writings he sees the political use of the law reduced to responsibility for the world, the Christian is left with even less indication of whether he is to build a socialist world, a capitalist world, an authoritarian or democratic world. The only criticism faith makes possible is the standing assertion that no political institution or decision is absolute: any concrete criticism must be the work of reason.

Looking back over Gogarten's early career as a whole, one is struck by the fact that the problem of history first posed for him by Ernst Troeltsch has been his central preoccupation. But it is a problem which has changed shape in various periods of Gogarten's development. At the beginning his uppermost concern was to assert the transcendence of God over against Troeltsch's immanentism. Growing naturally out of this critique came his concept of history as the encounter of Thou and I. Yet he was not satisfied to leave these encounters in the realm of chance meetings but sought to overcome the implied relativism of this view of history by reviving Luther's doctrine of the Orders of Creation. Yet even here he remained faithful to the basic insight of historicism when he granted that these "orders" are only relatively binding since their actual forms develop historically. At the time of the church struggle he went beyond the concept of the law as expressed in the concrete historical form of the orders and came to see the demand of the law in the *events* of history as well. His two works of 1948 form a kind of transition which reaches back to the Thou-I period in their emphasis on the relation to the neighbor and points forward to his idea that history is constituted by man's responsibility for the world (and his neighbor) before God. Thus Gogarten's early work shows a remarkable coherence of theme, a theme also common to Barth, Bultmann, and Brunner. Now that these men have made their major contribution to the resolution of the problem of faith and history, we may have the historical distance to begin a reappraisal of their original break with liberal theology on this issue. And in carrying out that reconsideration, Gogarten's early work on history will have to be taken into account.

BIBLIOGRAPHY

Works of Friedrich Gogarten

The following list includes all of Gogarten's major books and articles in chronological order. A complete bibliography up to 1962, prepared by Heinrich Runte, can be found in *Theologische Literaturzeitung*, LXXVII (1952), 745-48; LXXXVII (1962), 155-56. Between 1921 and 1928 most of the articles Gogarten wrote were assembled and published as four books; these articles have not been separately listed. Special mention must be made of the collection of essays from the early years of the "Dialectical Theology," edited by Jürgen Moltmann which contains several articles Gogarten published between 1920 and 1924: *Anfänge der dialektischen Theologie, Teil II, Rudolf Bultmann, Friedrich Gogarten, Eduard Thurneysen.* München: Christian Kaiser Verlag, 1963.

BOOKS

Fichte als religiöser Denker. Jena: Eugen Diederichs, 1914.

Religion und Volkstum (Tat-Flugschriften No. 5). Jena: Eugen Diederichs, 1915.

Religion weither. Jena: Eugen Diederichs, 1917.

Die religiöse Entscheidung. Jena: Eugen Diederichs, 1921.

Von Glauben und Offenbarung, Vier Vorträge. Jena: Eugen Diederichs, 1923.

Illusionen, Eine Auseinandersetzung mit dem Kulturidealismus. Jena: Eugen Diederichs, 1926.

223

The Secularization of History

Ich glaube an den dreieinigen Gott. Eine Untersuchung über Glaube und Geschichte. Jena: Eugen Diederichs, 1926.

Theologische Tradition und theologische Arbeit. Leipzig: J. C. Hinrichs'sche Buchhandlung, 1927.

Glaube und Wirklichkeit. Jena: Eugen Diederichs, 1928.

Die Schuld der Kirche gegen die Welt. Jena: Eugen Diederichs, 1928.

Wider die Ächtung der Autorität. Jena: Eugen Diederichs, 1930.

Politische Ethik. Jena: Eugen Diederichs, 1932.

Die Selbstverständlichkeiten unserer Zeit und der christliche Glaube. Berlin: Furche-Verlag, 1932. (Expanded and republished in 1937 as *Weltanschauung und Glaube.*)

Einheit von Evangelium und Volkstum? Hamburg: Hanseatische Verlagsanstalt, 1933.

Ist Volksgesetz Gottesgesetz? Hamburg: Hanseatische Verlagsanstalt, 1934.

Das Bekenntnis der Kirche. Jena: Eugen Diederichs, 1934.

Gericht oder Skepsis; Eine Streitschrift gegen Karl Barth. Jena: Eugen Diederichs, 1937.

Der Zerfall des Humanismus und die Gottesfrage. Stuttgart: Verlag W. Kohlhammer, 1937.

Die Verkündigung Jesu Christi. Heidelberg: Lambert Schneider, 1948.

Die Kirche in der Welt. Heidelberg: Lambert Schneider, 1948.

Der Mensch zwischen Gott und Welt, Eine Untersuchung über Gesetz und Evangelium. Heidelberg: Lambert Schneider, 1952. (Republished in 1956 by Friedrich Vorwerk, Stuttgart, without the subtitle.)

Entmythologisierung und Kirche. Stuttgart: Friedrich Vorwerk, 1953. (A second edition was published later the same year with an additional twelve page preface. The English translation, by Neville Horton Smith, *Demythologizing and History,* New York: Charles Scribner's Sons, 1955, is based on the first edition.)

Verhängnis und Hoffnung der Neuzeit, Die Säkularisierung als Theologisches Problem. Stuttgart: Friedrich Vorwerk, 1953.

Was ist Christentum? Göttingen: Vandenhoeck & Ruprecht, 1956.

Die Wirklichkeit des Glaubens; Zum Problem des Subjektivismus in der Theologie. Stuttgart, 1957. (English translation: *The Reality of Faith,* Philadelphia: The Westminster Press, 1959, tr. Carl Michalson *et al.*)

Der Schatz in irdenen Gefässen, Predigten. Stuttgart: Friedrich Vorwerk, 1960.

Jesus Christus Wende der Welt; Grundfragen der Christologie. Tübingen: J. C. B. Mohr, 1966.

ARTICLES

"Zwischen den Zeiten," *Die Christliche Welt,* XXXIV (1920), 374-78.

"Wider die romantische Theologie," *Die Christliche Welt,* XXXVI (1922), 514-19.

"Theologie und Wissenschaft: Grundsätzliche Bemerkungen zu Karl Holl's 'Luther,'" *Die Christliche Welt,* XXXVIII (1924), 34-42, 71-80, 121-22.

"Historismus," *Zwischen den Zeiten,* II (1924), 7-25.

"Das Gesetz und seine Erfüllung durch Jesus Christus," *Zwischen den Zeiten,* VI (1928), 368-83.

"Karl Barth's Dogmatik," *Theologische Rundschau,* Neue Folge I (1929), 60-80.

"Das Problem einer theologischen Anthropologie," *Zwischen den Zeiten,* VII (1929), 493-511.

"Wahrheit und Gewissheit," *Zwischen den Zeiten,* VIII (1930), 96-119.

"Die Krisis der Religion," *Zeitwende,* VII (1931), 22-38.

"Der Wahrheitsanspruch der Theologie," *Zeitschrift für Systematische Theologie,* IX (1931/32), 473-84.

"Menschheit und Gottheit Jesu Christi," *Zwischen den Zeiten,* X (1932), 3-21.

"Staat und Kirche," *Zwischen den Zeiten,* X (1932), 390-410.

"Schöpfung und Volkstum," *Zwischen den Zeiten,* X (1932), 481-504.

"Luther, der Theologe," *Deutsche Theologie,* I (1933), 1-10.

"Volkstum und Gottesgesetz," *Deutsche Theologie,* I (1934), 83-88.

"Die Bedeutung des ersten Gebotes für Kirche und Volk," *Deutsche Theologie,* I (1934), 283-93.

"Offenbarung und Geschichte," *Deutsche Theologie,* II (1935), 115-31.

"Altes und Neues Testament," *Deutsche Theologie,* II (1935), 199-213.

"Die Lehre von den zwei Reichen und das 'natürliche Gesetz,'" *Deutsche Theologie,* II (1935), 330-40.

"Wort Gottes und Schrift," *Deutsche Theologie,* III (1936), 197-219.

"Der doppelte Sinn von Gut und Böse, *Deutsche Theologie,* IV (1937), 330-45.

"Der Oeffentlichkeitscharakter der Kirche," *Evangelische Theologie,* VIII (1948/49), 343-50.

"Die christliche Wahrheit," *Festschrift für Rudolf Bultmann.* Stuttgart: W. Kohlhammer, 1949, pp. 84-98.

"Christlicher Glaube heute," *Zeitwende,* XX (1949), 345-59.

"Sittlichkeit und Glaube in Luthers Schrift *De servo arbitrio,"* *Zeitschrift für Theologie und Kirche,* XLVII (1950), 227-64.

"Entscheidung im Nichts," *Eckart,* Witten-Berlin, XXI (1952), 289-301.

The Secularization of History

"Theologie und Geschichte," *Zeitschrift für Theologie und Kirche,* L (1953), 339-94.

"Zur Frage nach dem Ursprung des geschichtlichen Denkens," *Evangelische Theologie,* XIV (1954), 226-38.

"Das abendländische Geschichtsdenken," *Zeitschrift für Theologie und Kirche,* LI (1954), 270-360. (English translation of 346-60 under the title "The Unity of History," *Theology Today,* XV (1958), 198-210.

"Schuld und Verantwortung der Theologie," *Zeit und Geschichte, Dankesgabe an Rudolf Bultmann zum 80. Geburtstag,* Erich Dinkler, ed., Tübingen: J. C. B. Mohr, 1964, pp. 461-66.

Works dealing with Friedrich Gogarten's theology

The following list is a selection of the more useful sources. Most of the works not listed date from before the Second World War.

BOOKS

Althaus, Paul. *The So-Called Kerygma and the Historical Jesus.* Tr. David Cairns. London: Oliver & Boyd, 1959.

Barth, Karl. *Church Dogmatics,* Vol. I, 1. Eds. G. W. Bromiley and T. F. Torrance. Edinburgh: T. & T. Clark, 1936.

Bonhoeffer, Dietrich. *Act and Being.* Tr. Bernard Noble. New York: Harper & Bros., 1961.

Brouillard, Henri. *Karl Barth: Genèse et évolution de la Théologie Dialectique.* Paris: Aubier, 1957.

Diem, Hermann. *Dogmatics.* Tr. Harold Knight. Edinburgh: Oliver & Boyd, 1959.

Fuchs, Ernst. *Begegnung mit dem Wort. Eine Rede für Friedrich Gogarten.* Bad Cannstatt: R. Müllerschön, 1955.

——*Hermeneutik.* Bad Cannstatt; R. Müllerschön, 1954.

Kinder, Ernst. *Das neuzeitliche Geschichtsdenken und die Theologie, Antwort an Friedrich Gogarten.* Berlin: Lutherisches Verlagshaus, 1954.

Langmeyer, Bernard. *Der Dialogische Personalismus in der evangelischen und katholischen Theologie der Gegenwart.* Paderborn: Bonifacius-Druckerei, 1963.

Merz, Georg. *Wege und Wandlungen, Erinnerungen aus der Zeit von 1892-1922.* München: Christian Kaiser, 1961.

Noller, Gerhard. *Sein und Existenz.* München: Christian Kaiser, 1962.

Pannenberg, Wolfhart. *Offenbarung als Geschichte.* Göttingen: Vandenhoeck & Ruprecht, 1961.

Bibliography

Rietveld, B. *Saecularisatie als Probleem der Theologische Ethiek.* 's-Gravenhage: Keulen, no date.

Schilling, S. Paul. *Contemporary Continental Theologians.* Nashville: Abingdon Press, 1966.

Soedarmo, R., *In de wereld maar niet van de wereld.* Kampen: J. H. Kok, 1957.

Strohm, Theodor. *Konservative politische Romantik in den theologischen Frühschriften Friedrich Gogartens.* Berlin: Freie Universität Berlin, 1961.

Wagler, Roland. *Der Ort der Ethik bei Friedrich Gogarten.* Hamburg-Bergstedt: Herbert Reich, Evangelischer Verlag, 1961.

ARTICLES

Brandenburg, Albert, "Glaube und Geschichte bei Friedrich Gogarten," *Münchener theologische Zeitschrift,* VI (1955), 319-34.

Bultmann, Rudolf. "The Historicity of Man and Faith," *Existence and Faith,* Schubert M. Ogden, ed. (New York: Meridian Books, 1960) pp. 92-110. (German original published in 1930.)

Fuchs, Ernst. "Entmythologisierung und Säkularisierung," *Theologische Literaturzeitung,* LXXIX (1954), 723-32.

Gloege, Gerhard. "Der theologische Personalismus als dogmatisches Problem," *Kerygma und Dogma,* I (1955), 23-41.

Holl, Karl. "Gogarten's Lutherauffassung: Eine Erwiderung," *Die Christliche Welt,* XXXVIII (1924), 307-14.

Ittel, G. W. "Sein und Existenz: Eine Auseinandersetzung mit G. Nollers gleichnamigem Buch im Hinblick auf die Theologie Friedrich Gogartens," *Zeitschrift für Theologie und Kirche,* LX (1963), 349-69.

Joest, Wilfried. " 'Verhängnis und Hoffnung der Neuzeit': Kritische Gedanken zu Friedrich Gogartens Buch," *Kerygma und Dogma,* I (1955), 70-83.

Kamlah, Wilhelm. "Gilt es wirklich 'die Entscheidung zwischen geschichtlichem und metaphysischem Denken'?" *Evangelische Theologie,* XIV (1954), 171-77.

Kreck, Walter. "Die Christologie Gogartens und ihre Weiterführung in der heutigen Frage nach dem historischen Jesus," *Evangelische Theologie,* XXIII (1963), 169-97.

McConnachie, John. "The Barthian School, III, Friedrich Gogarten," *Expository Times,* XLIII (1931/32) 391-93, 461-65.

Ott, Heinrich. "Objectification and Existentialism," *Kerygma and Myth,* II (London: S.P.C.K., 1962), 306-35.

Pannenberg, Wolfhart. "Heilsgeschehen und Geschichte," *Kerygma und Dogma,* V (1959), 218-37, 259-88.

Prenter, Regin. "Das Evangelium der Säkularisierung. Bemerkungen zu Friedrich Gogartens letzten Werken," *Theologische Zeitschrift,* XII (1956), 605-30.

Runyon, Theodore. "Friedrich Gogarten," *A Handbook of Christian Theologians,* Martin E. Marty and D. G. Peerman, eds. (Cleveland: World, 1965), pp. 427-44.

Scholder, Klaus. "Neuere deutsche Geschichte und protestantische Theologie, *Evangelische Theologie,* XXIII (1963), 510-36.

Troeltsch, Ernst. "Ein Apfel vom Baume Kierkegaards," *Die Christliche Welt,* XXXV (1921), 186-89.

Index

Absolute, 62, 198

Action, 45, 53, 129, 132, 146, 148, 150, 151, 153, 166, 172, 184, 185; *see also* Being

Activity, 28, 48, 76, 91, 113, 129, 150, 172, 187

Anthropology, 22-23, 83, 201-3

Apologetics, 174, 187

Aron, Raymond, 60

Aseity, 44-45, 51, 56

Auerbach, Erich, 37

Authority, 204-5, 211, 220

Autonomy, 32, 39, 42-43, 51-52, 57, 148, 152, 167-68, 180, 182, 204, 209, 217, 219

Barth, Karl, 17, 21, 70, 81, 183, 193, 196-97, 199, 200-203, 208, 214-16, 219

Being, 21, 129, 131, 146, 151, 154, 160, 172, 185, 187
and act, 172, 187
being-for-the-other, 154, 205
being-from-the-other, 154, 205-6, 218
of God, 130

Being—*cont'd*
being-in-the-world, 71
inversion of, 96, 101-5, 110, 155
of man, 31, 54, 56, 96, 107, 130, 159, 180
out of God, 31, 33, 91-92, 99, 100, 103, 134, 142, 160
as person, 34, 102, 104, 156
of world, 130, 177, 180

Bible
approach to history in, 66-67
inspiration of, 135-36

Bond, 45-46, 148, 152, 153, 156. 169-70, 204-5, 211

Bonhoeffer, Dietrich, 17, 18, 70, 174, 182

Bonus, Arthur, 192

Boundary, 45, 80, 152, 164, 168, 170, 213

Brunner, Emil, 17, 81, 196-97, 206-7, 219

Buber, Martin, 65, 183, 199-200

Bultmann, Rudolf, 21, 70-72, 86-90, 115, 119, 145-46, 182, 197, 201, 219

229

Call, 71, 99, 127-28, 130-32, 142, 154

Chalcedon, 106-7

Christianity, 41, 218
and Christian faith, 39-41, 164-65
as world view, 36, 40, 165

Christology, 19, 20, 79, 81, 83, 100, 105-17, 181, 201

Church, 36, 38, 42, 45, 133-36, 138, 160-61, 181, 207, 216, 219
as community of the Word, 135, 160, 163-64, 173
medieval, 37, 47
solidarity with world, 160, 164
visible and invisible, 160-61, 163, 172-73

Church struggle, 192, 215-16, 220

Confessing Church, 208, 215

Conservative revolution, 209-11, 216

Community, 56, 211; see also Church

Conscience, 46, 123, 166, 184, 198

Cosmic powers, 27-28, 33-34, 38-39, 45, 96, 132, 166, 168

Cosmos, 27, 31, 38, 175-76

Counterpart, 31, 46, 48, 217

Courage, 22, 78, 81, 167-68

Cox, Harvey, 19, 157, 182-84

Creation, 62-63, 77, 133, 163, 177

Crisis, 192, 195, 197, 209

Cross, 35, 86-87, 99, 101, 103-4, 105, 109, 115, 123, 124, 132, 135, 137, 139, 145, 155, 185

Crucifixion, 102-4

Culture, 166-67, 195, 197, 209

Curse, 103

Death, 56, 103, 105, 109, 116

Debt; see Guilt

Decision, 62, 63, 94, 118, 125 ff., 128, 132, 161, 186, 200, 210-11

Demythologizing, 21

Desacralization, 35, 40, 48, 175-76, 210

Dependence, 168; see also Directedness

Descartes, René, 39, 42

Destiny, 34, 94-95, 97-98, 103, 105, 111, 116-17, 152, 210

Dialectical theology, 191, 197

Diederichs, Eugen, 193

Diem, Hermann, 108

Dilthey, Wilhelm, 71

Directedness, 57, 69, 125

Ebeling, Gerhard, 18, 88, 115, 121, 182

Ebner, Ferdinand, 199

Eliade, Mircea, 175-76

Ellwein, Eduard, 119

Empiricism, 180, 189

Encounter, 44, 64-65, 67, 93, 159, 198, 200, 220

Enlightenment, 36, 47, 210, 218

Eschatology, 67-68, 71, 73

Eternity, 106-10, 111, 216

Ethics, 19, 151, 153, 161, 170, 173, 181, 206
biblical, 149, 169, 212, 219
Christian, 40-41, 149, 151, 159, 164
contextualist, 169-71
political, 204-7, 219
see also Law

Existentialism, 21, 113, 189

Fact, 19, 118, 137-41, 146

Faith, 22, 48, 62, 79, 83, 93, 105, 115, 123, 143, 152, 164, 181
  act of, 117, 119, 126-27
  as courage, 78
  decision of, 125-33, 150
  as distinguishing, 128-29, 150, 152
  as freedom, 48, 132, 167-68, 187
  object of, 119-22, 126-27, 132
  as perception, 126-27, 129, 130, 139, 144
  reality of, 118-19, 124-25, 132, 138-42
  as remaining, 127-28, 131
  subject of, 119, 126
  and works, 149-52, 170-71, 186

Fall, 30-31

Fate, 36, 92, 98, 167-68, 194

Fateful entanglement, 96, 98, 101-3, 110, 113, 114, 117, 124, 169

Figural interpretation, 37

First World War, 192-94, 209

Forgiveness, 56, 65, 161

Freedom, 22, 26, 43, 46, 48, 51, 56, 73, 119, 122, 128, 141, 142, 155, 162, 167-68, 190, 204, 210-11, 217, 218, 219
  from cosmic powers, 28, 32, 34, 45, 117, 139, 147, 149, 150
  for God, 32, 38, 78, 91, 152, 153, 172, 185
  for world, 38, 132, 153, 184; see also Faith

Fuchs, Ernst, 18, 115, 121, 182

Future, 67, 146
  anticipation of, 68-70, 122, 124, 168, 185
  impenetrable and oncoming, 53, 67-69, 74-75, 78-80, 101, 109, 111, 116, 119, 121, 124-25, 132, 142, 157, 165, 168, 185
  mystery of, 81, 122, 125, 152
  proximate, 68, 74, 152, 165, 167, 185

German Christians, 208, 213-14, 215

God, 28-30, 40, 43-44, 62, 64, 67, 70, 120, 122, 130, 137, 150, 156, 207, 213
  the Creator, 31, 50-51, 62, 65, 124, 133, 151, 212
  death of, 17, 74-75, 181
  existence of, 75, 76
  as Father, 101, 107-11, 112, 140
  for us, 80, 110, 127, 156, 177
  hiddenness of, 52, 54, 67, 70, 74-78, 79, 80, 102, 120
  in himself, 80, 110
  knowledge of, 77-78, 110
  as mystery, 30, 42, 44, 52-54, 75-76, 78, 81, 93, 99-100, 112, 115, 119, 124, 126, 127, 131, 134, 138, 144, 149, 162, 165, 173, 177
  oncoming futurity of, 67-68, 74, 81, 93-94, 153
  power of, 51, 75, 78, 81, 111, 113, 121, 124, 125, 130-31, 151
  question of, 49, 51-58, 61, 74, 78, 195

God—*Cont'd*
  term, 51, 74-75
  who makes alive the dead, 32,
    77, 81, 103, 105, 120, 130,
    132, 168, 178
  wrath of, 102-3, 105, 110, 116
Gospel, 72-73, 78
Goss, James, 146
Grace, 112, 115, 139, 142, 150,
    161, 207
Greeks, 27, 32, 34, 46, 66
Grisebach, Eberhard, 199-200
Guilt, 56, 65, 132, 142, 155, 194,
    217
Gusdorf, Georges, 27

Hare, R. M., 180
Hamilton, William, 20, 180-81
Harnack, Adolf von, 192
Hebrews, 34, 36
Heidegger, Martin, 42-43, 47, 55,
    70-72, 100, 142
Hellenistic philosophy, 36, 40,
    46-47, 140
Hermeneutics, 72, 198
Herrmann, Wilhelm, 115, 139,
    199
Hitler, Adolf, 208
Historian, 141
Historical
  construction, 60-61
  development, 194, 198
  explanation, 58-61, 63, 79
  narrative, 60, 66
  proof, 144-46
  reality, 58-69, 73, 79, 119, 138-
    42, 145-46, 185-86, 188-89
  research, 58-61, 79, 90, 133,
    136-41, 143, 144-46, 188
  truth, 203

Historicism, 197-98
Historicity, 37, 66, 70
  of God, 51
  of man, 49, 58, 61, 81, 189
  of revelation, 18, 68
Historicization, 18, 34, 46, 48-49,
    71, 72, 106, 175-76, 197
History, 19, 20, 27, 34, 58, 60,
    75, 81, 108, 112, 167-68, 188,
    221
  concept of, 58-70, 188, 197-98,
    200, 220
  density of, 66-67, 94, 112
  divine and human, 107-11,
    186-87
  external, 144-46
  internal, 145-46
  meaning of, 57-59, 61, 138, 140
  philosophy of, 58-59, 138, 197
  see also Secularization
Holl, Karl, 199, 201
Holy Spirit, 72, 135-36
Humanism, 196, 210
Humanity, 51, 57, 65, 217

Idealism, 191-94, 197-98, 200,
    202
Ideology, 54, 76, 165, 166, 199
Independence, 26, 28, 34, 36, 39,
    42-43, 46, 48, 150, 152, 168,
    177, 185, 218-19
Individualism, 85, 193, 213, 218,
    219
Individuality, 32, 193
Inheritance, 32, 44, 102, 111, 127
Intention, 120-21, 133-34, 136,
    138
Israel, 91, 100
I-Thou, 62, 65, 183, 199-200,
    201; *see also* Thou-I

Jesus Christ, 33, 41, 77-78, 81, 84-117, 155, 193, 212
  destiny of, 101, 113-14, 139
  difference from other men, 85-86, 111, 113
  divinity of, 84, 113, 115
  faith of, 89, 97-99, 133, 146
  form of existence, 91, 95
  historical, 88-89, 107, 114
  historical reality of, 63-64, 83, 88-90, 120, 123, 132, 162, 187, 203
  humanity of, 84-87, 104, 106, 109, 113, 115, 122
  nothing of himself, 101, 114, 115
  obedience of, 87, 97, 99-100, 103, 111, 114, 116, 137, 146
  person of, 86-87, 104, 109-10, 112, 124, 132, 143, 146
  preaching of, 66, 83, 87, 91-95, 97, 99, 101, 111
  responsibility before God, 96-97, 109, 111-12
  responsibility for the world, 97, 100, 103, 110-12, 133, 137, 146
  sending of, 100-101
  solidarity with sinners, 64, 95-97
  work of, 104-5, 116; *see also* Son of God, Sonship
John the Baptist, 97
John, Gospel of, 100-101
Judaism, 27, 41, 46
Judgment, 68, 159, 195
Jünger, Ernst, 210
Justification, 165, 166
  by faith, 33, 39, 74, 150, 170-71, 181

Justification—*Cont'd*
  by works, 45, 163, 168-69, 171, 184

Kamlah, Wilhelm, 108
Kerygma, 87-90, 99, 103, 133, 134, 138-39, 146
Kierkegaard, Sören, 140, 193
Kinder, Ernst, 119
Kingdom of God, 92, 95-96, 98, 100-101
Knowledge, 28, 36, 54, 69, 77, 110, 117, 124, 131, 159, 203
Krüger, Gerhard, 118
Kutter, Hermann, 192

Lagarde, Paul de, 210
Langbehn, Julius, 210
Law, 26, 29, 33, 56, 72-74, 122, 136, 148, 150, 152, 160, 162, 166, 171, 214, 219, 220
  fulfillment of, 33, 52, 92
  and Gospel, 52-54, 73, 77, 82, 183-85, 212-13, 215-16
  natural, 45, 149, 169-70, 219
  two uses of, 52-53, 212-13
Liberalism, 84, 174, 191, 193, 194, 196, 199-200, 210, 217, 221
Littell, Franklin, 209
Love, 56, 92-93, 102, 105, 116, 153-56, 157, 172
Luther, Martin, 36, 38-39, 47, 75, 106, 122, 125, 130, 151, 157, 158, 163, 185, 189, 193-95, 199, 207, 220

MacLeish, Archibald, 51
MacQuarrie, John, 21

The Secularization of History

Man, 30-31, 51, 54, 57-58, 60, 61, 65, 74, 76; *see also* Being, Humanity
Mann, Thomas, 210
Marcel, Gabriel, 55
Maritain, Jacques, 178-79
Maturity, 26, 33-34, 36, 40, 51, 192, 203
Meaning, 57, 64, 66, 69, 103, 119, 162, 166
Mehl, Roger, 68
Merz, Georg, 192, 196
Metaphysics, 20, 38, 40, 100, 106, 116, 143, 182, 189
Michalson, Carl, 19, 21, 180, 182
Middle Ages, 35, 47
Moeller van den Bruck, Arthur, 210
Moralism, 40, 43, 171, 182
Morality, 148, 211
Mystery, 41, 56, 65, 75, 106, 130, 148, 181, 182
  absolute, 69, 74, 79-80, 92, 93, 115, 132, 162, 164-65, 178
  concept of, 55-57
  divine; *see* God
  of existence, 28, 32, 43, 53, 57, 102, 128, 131, 140, 159, 164, 166, 167, 180
  of world, 57, 162, 163, 166, 180
Myth, 27, 73; *see also* World

Nationalism, 208, 218
Nationality, 193, 211, 215
National Socialism, 18, 208-9, 216, 218
Nature, 19, 40, 58, 81, 177, 189
Neighbor, 62, 64, 80, 93, 95, 96, 111, 146, 149, 151, 153-56, 164, 181, 213, 220

Niebuhr, H. R., 179
Nietzsche, Friedrich, 50, 55, 210
Nihilism, 123, 159, 166
Nothingness, 55-56, 81, 105, 115-16, 123-24, 126-27, 132, 142, 144, 154, 177

Obedience, 126, 139; *see also* Jesus Christ
Objectivity, 42-43, 58, 116, 118, 140
Obligation, 56, 204-5, 211
Ong, Walter J., 175
Openness, 22, 34-35, 67, 78, 93-94, 104, 113, 122, 132, 146, 154-56, 165, 168
Order, 30, 45, 147-48, 152, 158, 165, 171, 206
Orders, 169-71, 204-5, 207, 211
Orthodoxy, 39, 47, 72, 202, 213

Participation, 29, 99, 139, 198
Past, 62-64, 67, 79, 138
Paul, 27, 31, 33, 38, 41, 45-47, 87, 91
Personhood, 28-32, 40, 43-44, 123, 127, 132, 134, 150, 153, 156, 171
Personality, 43-44, 86, 90, 193
Person, 28, 86-87, 111, 114, 121, 159
Phenomenology, 19, 80, 189
Politics; *see* Ethics, Order
Positions, 157-58, 204, 207
Preaching, 133-35, 163-64
Prenter, Regin, 20
Profane, 176, 179
Progress, 45, 159
Providence, 37

Race, 211-12

Rade, Martin, 194

Ragaz, Leonnard, 192

Reality, 51, 75, 93, 119, 127, 128-29, 130-31, 138, 147, 156, 182, 184-85, 188, 198, 199

Reason, 34, 38, 47, 152-53, 159, 164, 170, 213

Receptivity, 28, 42, 48, 91-92, 103-4, 113, 128-29, 150-51, 153, 172, 187, 205

Relativism, 59, 198, 205, 219-20

Religion, 30-31, 165, 191, 195, 197-99, 209

Religious Socialism, 194

Ritschl, Albrecht, 201

Renaissance, 26, 39, 47

Response, 28-29, 57, 79, 131, 135, 138, 142, 150-51, 158, 164, 177, 207

Responsibility, 27, 39, 56-57, 67, 72, 91, 114, 119, 150, 154, 157, 159, 162, 166, 168, 171, 184, 189-90, 193-94, 205, 207, 217

before God, 31-32

before the world, 31, 101

concept of, 29, 65, 157

inversion of, 101-2, 122

for the world, 18, 29, 32, 34-36, 40, 46, 53, 65, 69, 71, 74, 76-77, 117, 124, 128, 132, 142, 148, 153, 156, 168-69, 177, 190, 219, 220

see also Jesus Christ

Resurrection, 86-87, 99, 101, 103-5, 111, 123-24, 132, 135, 137, 139, 185

Revelation, 19, 70-71, 78, 85,

Revelation—Cont'd
115-16, 119, 124, 129, 132, 138, 143, 185, 188, 212, 216

Robinson, James M., 88

Sacred, 28, 48, 76, 179; see also Profane

Salvation; see Wholeness

Sanctification, 179

Schleiermacher, Friedrich, 113-14, 201-2

Scholastic theology, 37

Schopenhauer, Arthur, 210

Science, 26, 36, 39-40, 54, 57, 60, 138-40, 167, 178

Second World War, 18, 22

Secular, 19, 48, 50, 162-63, 167, 217

Secularism, 166-68, 180, 184, 196

Secularity, 32, 167, 170

Secularization, 17-18, 22, 38, 46, 49, 148, 158, 165 ff., 174 ff., 179, 182, 185, 189-92, 203, 209, 211, 218

of Christianity, 41, 164-65

Christian origin of, 18-20, 27-35, 46

concept of, 25-26, 35, 41-46, 47-48

delay of, 35-40, 46-47

of ethics, 147-48

of history, 18, 34-35, 189

modern form of, 41-45

Sin, 31-32, 123-24, 162, 177

Socialism, 196, 220

Son of God, 100-101, 104-5, 107-11, 113, 140

Sonship

Jesus', 100, 105, 110, 112, 127

Sonship—*Cont'd*
  man's, 32-34, 80, 100, 111, 124, 128
  mature, 40, 43, 91
Spengler, Oswald, 210
Stallmann, Martin, 25
State, 45, 205, 207-8, 214, 218
Subject-object problem, 42, 50, 61, 72, 119, 130, 188
Subject-ism, 42, 47, 54, 119
Subjectivism, 21, 42-44, 48, 54, 65, 72, 131, 169, 181, 185, 197
Subjectivity, 46, 129, 131-32
Superhistory, 20, 59, 62, 137, 143, 170
Supernatural, 20, 37, 40, 90, 103, 143, 154, 186, 189

Taub, Gottfried, 192
Technology, 34, 54, 57-58, 69, 74, 147-48, 157-58, 160, 167, 177, 182, 183
Theology
  and anthropology, 201-3
  "historical," 20, 38, 106, 114, 116, 185-89
  method, 22, 52, 70-72, 82, 141, 188-89, 201-2
  natural, 73, 81-83
  task of, 51, 53-54, 70-71, 73-74, 188, 197
Thou-I, 29, 62-65, 67, 70, 79, 193, 199-200, 219-20;
  see also I-Thou
Thurneysen, Eduard, 196-97, 201
Tillich, Paul, 183
Time, 106-10, 216

Tolstoy, Leo, 192
Tradition, 135, 159
Transcendence, 59, 178, 220
Trinity, 106
Troeltsch, Ernst, 41, 60-61, 71, 197-98, 200, 219-20
Trust, 56, 65, 92, 95, 103-4, 129, 154

Van Buren, Paul, 20, 180-82
Volk, 211-12, 214-16, 218

Wieman, Henry Nelson, 17
Weimar Republic, 208-9, 213
Wholeness, 45, 54, 57, 69, 101, 106, 111, 129, 163, 178, 181
Winter, Gibson, 157, 183
Witness, 123-24, 134-36, 138
Wittgenstein, Ludwig, 55
Word
  answering, 29, 121, 135
  of God, 29, 52, 73, 77, 80, 82-83, 99, 121, 130, 134-35, 155, 160-62, 164, 182, 197-98, 216
  immediate, 29, 121-23, 132-33, 135
Works; *see* Faith, Justification
World, 100
  care of, 32-33, 158
  concept of, 29-30
  "existing," 94, 97, 146
  man's relation to, 26, 27-28, 54
  mythical relation to, 27, 35
  "personal," 94-95, 98, 146
  see also Responsibility
World view, 36-37, 39-40, 48, 72

Zwischen den Zeiten, 196-97

DATE DUE

GAYLORD — PRINTED IN U.S.A.